THE NEW MODERN
FURNITURE DESIGN

Whitney Library of Design
An imprint of Watson-Guptill Publications
New York

THE NEW MODERN
FURNITURE DESIGN

Whitney

AUTHOR
Francisco Asensio Cerver

DESIGN & LAYOUT
Estudio Gráfico Arco

© Francisco Asensio Cerver. 1998

PUBLISHED BY
Whitney Library of Design
An imprint of Watson-Guptill Publications
New York

ISBN: 0-8230-7194-4

Printed in Spain
Gràfiques Ibèria, S.A.

CONTENTS

"The connections, the connections, it will in the end be these details that give the product its life".

Frederick S. Wright Gallery, University of California.
Connections; The Work of Charles and Ray Eames.
UCLA Arts Council. Loa Angeles 1976. P.48

"Eventually everything connects people, ideas, objects, etc., the quality of the connections is the key to quality per se".

J&M Neuchart & R. Eames
Eames Design: The Work of the Office of Charles and Ray Eames Harry
N.Abrams, NY 1989. P266

THE CREATIVE PROCESS   AN INTRODUCTION

"When I think of a story, the first thing that comes to my mind is an image that for some reason seems to be loaded with meaning, even though I may not be able to express this meaning in discursive or conceptual terms. As soon as this image is sufficiently clear in my mind, I start to develop it into a story. Perhaps it might be more accurate to say that the images themselves develop their implicit potential, the story that they contain within. Each image generates another, forming a collection of analogies, symmetries, and contrasts. The visual and conceptual organization of this material is where my intentions come into play. My job is to put the story in order and make it understandable, or perhaps to try and establish which of the meanings are compatible with the general thrust of the story and which are not, always leaving a certain number of possible options."

Italo Calvino, *Six Proposals for the Next Millennium*

S If we replace the word object with story in the fragment above from Italo Calvino, it is easy to see that creativity has certain common mechanisms and universal rules that are independent of specific forms of creativity, such as literature, music, painting, sculpture, or design. Calvino describes how an image comes to his mind and weaves a web of relationships that finally allow him to create a story or work of literature.

The way a designer approaches an object is similar, although there are small yet definite differences that affect the creative process in each case. The most important of these differences is that the designer usually works with the customer. A person who orders the design and specifies the theme and framework in which the creative process must take place. The manufacturer is the starting point in the creative process, the person who is responsible for carrying the project along until the first meaningful images appear in the designer's mind.

The creative process can vary substantially from one project to another. In some cases the image is created in advance, while in other cases it is merely a rough, fuzzy concept that needs to be verified by several three-dimensional models and prototypes. In this sense, design is similar to architecture in that it relies on a process of trial and error.

The designer lives between two worlds that touch and yet reject one another, the world of the subjective and that of the objective. The first world is based on symbols, originality, and the relatively immutable intrinsic nature of objects. It is connected to the magic of creativity, the influence of history and memory, and the great masters and visionaries of the field of design. The second world is the real world, which is related to markets, investments, costs, the manufacturer, and the production schedule. One world represents desires; the other, reality. From this point of view, the closer our desires are to reality, the better the design will be.

The ability of an object to stir emotions, to attract, and to seduce has little to do with the materials it is made of, the use it is put to, its size, or its manufacturer. It comes from a coherent process of development, where desires cannot be betrayed by reality and where the connection between worlds of the subjective and the objective remains unbroken and intact.

Jorge Pensi

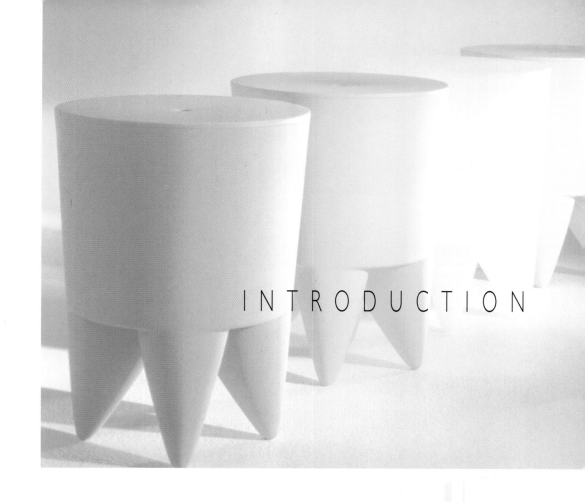

We live in an age when design is invading all aspects of life, imposing its fads and fashions. Design is present not only in exquisite luxury items such as jewelry, adornments, and works of art, but also in the most simple, common, and practical objects for everyday use. Nowadays, it is not enough for an object to do its job efficiently; it must also do it with style. Even the simplest household objects are expected to be at least attractive, if not beautiful.

As design marches boldly and often insolently into every area of life, it pushes aside traditional notions of beauty and taste, transforming visual criteria. Nowhere is this trend more apparent than in the field of interior design. Furniture is rapidly and inexorably changing, fulfilling new needs and changing the style and appearance of interior spaces.

As a witness to this inevitable change, and as a passionate admirer and observer of interior design, the author has tried to collect the many different trends in modern furniture design in one volume. Modern Furniture Design is the result of this desire.

This volume covers a broad range of pieces, including tables, chairs, sofas, armchairs, bookcases, closets, and cabinets. There are designs for every taste. On one hand, there are classical pieces that have been brought up to date to meet modern needs and tastes. At the opposite end of the spectrum there are revolutionary, avant-garde designs that are unlike anything before.

The latest designs for tables include pieces with a strong, imposing presence inspired by the rustic tradition. Others shock and delight the observer with their wavy, imaginative shapes and twisted legs that seem to defy the dictates of common sense. Still others strive for utmost simplicity, avoiding any unnecessary adornments. This minimalist approach is also exemplified by the materials used. Many pieces are made of plate glass or other light, airy materials.

Modern chairs tend to be svelte, graceful pieces that can often be stacked for easy storage. Due to their simple minimalist designs, many of them look like garden or office furniture. Many of the materials used in their construction are new, such as plant fiber. Other materials, such as plastic, have recovered prestige after being out of style for some time. The most popular and prestigious material, however, is still wood.

DUAL-PURPOSED FURNITURE

12

In small apartments convertible furniture is an essential aspect of decor. These practical pieces are real space-savers that do the jobs of two pieces of furniture while only taking up the space of one. The most common piece of dual-purpose furniture is the sofa-bed. However, until recently, these pieces were unsatisfactory in all of their functions; they made uncomfortable sofas, uncomfortable beds, and unattractive pieces of furniture. The newest models guarantee a maximum of comfort and make an attractive addition to the decor of any house.

The Prao sofa, designed by Peter Maly, easily makes the change from sofa to bed thanks to an exceptionally simple mechanism. All that is needed is to fold down one of the armrests. As a sofa, this piece is impeccably designed. It features a metal frame, and its comfortable body consists of one seamless cushion. Its back and armrests are large cushions upholstered in striped material. Both armrests can be folded down.

Sofas, however, are not the only pieces of furniture that can change into beds. The Tango chair, by V. Laprell and T. Althaus, can be easily changed into a single bed. When closed, Tango is a charming and inviting armchair that surrounds the body with its warm, softly padded surfaces. A simple pull on one of its armrests transforms it into a comfortable single bed.

1 The Prao sofa-bed.
2 The Tango armchair.
3 The Tosca sofa-bed.
4 The Tosca sofa-bed opens to form two twin beds.
5 The Tango armchair.

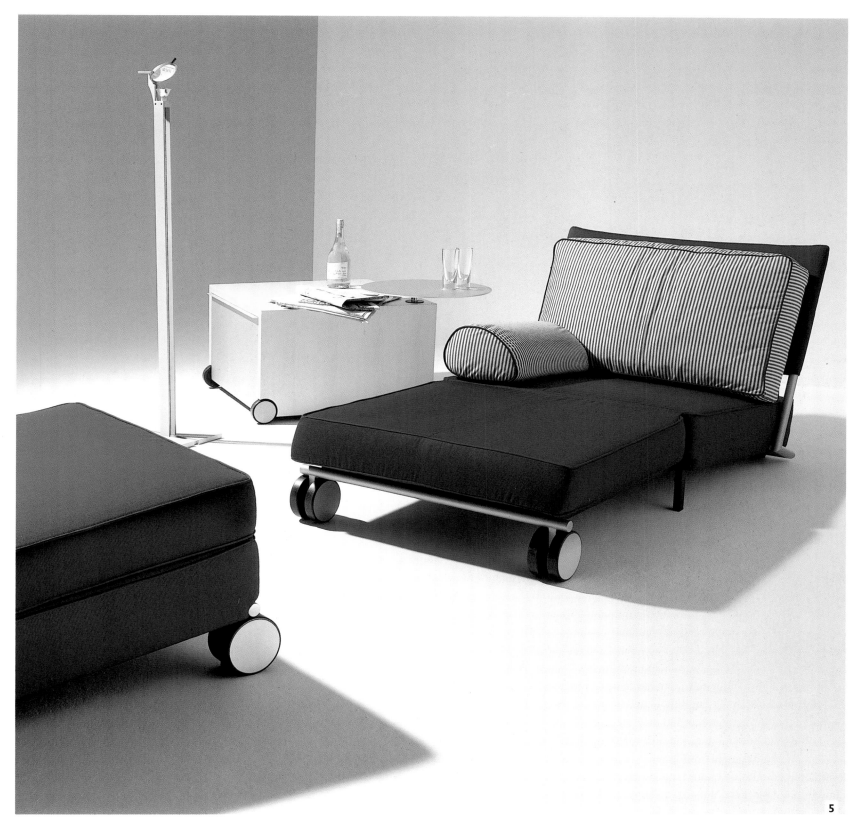

13

5

The Tosca sofa, designed by T. Althaus, takes advantage of the entire surfaces of its seat and back to change into a pair of twin beds, connected in the middle. The model is characterized by its serene elegance and exquisitely balanced design. Thanks to these characteristics, the Tosca sofa easily blends into a wide range of decorative styles.

The last model dealt with here is the Trinus chair, which can change into a distinguished chaise longue or a bed, as needed. This piece features front wheels, and its body is padded with thick, comfortable cushions.

FOR ALL TASTES

An upholstered chair is a piece of furniture that easily adapts to any time or place. Its shape can become soft and rounded or sharp and angular according to the dictates of fashion. Stain-resistant synthetic fibers take the place of traditional materials, and bright colors come to the foreground.

Among the selected models is the Palio chair, made by Kron from a Jorge Pensi design. Its compact size makes it ideal for small spaces, but what makes it stand out is its strong personality, due in large part to its elegant, cone-shaped legs. The legs are available in four finishes: natural, cherry, mahogany, and black. The supporting structure is made of wood, and the cushions and back are padded with polyurethane foam in various densities, and are covered with Dacron.

The last model illustrated on these pages is the Flavia armchair, designed by J. L. Pérez for Kron. Its structure consists of a one-piece frame made of injected rigid polyurethane. The arms and back are filled with foam rubber, which was injected and left to cool. The legs that support this charming armchair are made of wood, and are available in natural, cherry, mahogany, and black finishes.

The Flavia armchair stands out because of its comfortable rounded shape, specially designed to provide back support. In addition, its brightly colored upholstery makes it ideal for young people. The Flavia collection also includes three sofas, all with solid wood seats and backs padded with polyurethane foam in various densities and covered with Dacron. The arms of the sofas are made of rigid polyurethane and are part of the frame.

The other piece shown is the chair from the Decó collection, designed by Torstein Nilsen for Andreu World, S. A. It is characterized by its strong, straight lines and comes with or without arms. The seat and back can be upholstered in different colors, which opens up a myriad of decorative possibilities. The Decó collection also includes a model with curved lines.

1 Chair from the Palio collection.
2 Decó chair with straight lines.
3 Decó chair with rounded lines.
4 Flavia chair

4

LIGHTING AND DESIGN

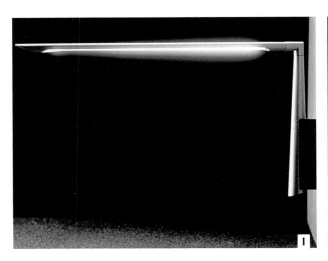

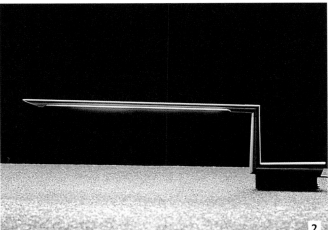

Lamps and other lighting fixtures perform a dual function in interior design: besides providing direct or indirect light for a room, they can be attractive and esthetically pleasing in themselves. A well designed lamp is like a sculpture. Lamps and other lighting fixtures should attract attention as much for their design as for their function.

On the these two pages there are lighting designs for every taste. Some are so simple and discreet that their impact is very subtle, whereas others are larger, more elaborate, and constitute a more obvious part of the room's decoration. The first two lamps are different versions of the Eliana model, created by the Spanish designer M. Ybargüengoitia. It is made of brass and zamack and uses a 13-watt fluorescent tube, 7 millimeters in diameter.

The next lighting fixture, Weighted Lamp, designed by Pete Sans, is considered a classic. This ceiling lamp has a pulley adjusts its height. The weight and wall separator are made of graphite, while the frame of the lampshade is made of steel and painted white. The lampshade, which is made of linen, is available in two shapes: cylindrical (for one bulb) or oval (for two).

The Tronkonil design is based on the simple, elegant shape of a cone. The lamp is comprised of three pieces: a central cone with its widest mouth facing upward, and two smaller cones that emerge from each end of the central piece. It is especially appropriate for indirect or complementary lighting.

The sculptural quality of these lamps is apparent in the Dualada model by the Disseny Blanc Studio. Its wide surface and elliptical design make it a unique and decorative piece, ideal for illuminating any corner of the house.

Finally, there is the daring and innovative design of the Winston fixture, by the Japanese designer J. Daifuku. This singular lamp can be used on either the wall or the ceiling. It is made of brass with a gray finish and uses a fluorescent tube.

1 The Eliana wall fixture..
2 The Eliana desktop model.
3 Weighted Lamp.
4 The Tronkonil.
5 The Dualada.
6 The Winston.

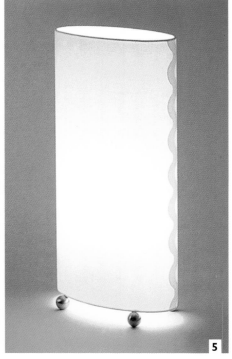

16

PRACTICAL RESTING PLACES

Tatamis are comfortable platforms designed to hold a mattress. They have been enjoyed by several generations in Japan, and are currently being adopted by more and more people in the West, who have come to prefer the comfort and efficiency of the tatami to their traditional bed frames and box springs.

Tatamis are fastened to the headboard by sliding rails, so that they can be easily moved from one part of the room to another when the need arises. For example, a king-sized bed can be divided into two single beds. This can be useful when one person is sick or wants to read without disturbing the other.

These practical beds, in addition to being ideal for sleeping and relaxing, are a paradigm of harmony that results from an exquisite combination of shapes, materials and colors. The design of a tatami is perfection itself, and tatamis can be the ideal way to divide a room into well-proportioned spaces. They bring movement to a room and help solve the many spatial problems that can arise in a bedroom. For instance, in a small bedroom a tatami can be moved next to the window during the day to allow more free space for other activities. They also facilitate cleaning, since they can slide easily to one side to allow cleaning under the bed.

The head of the bed is made up of sliding panels that reveal a large number of shelves and drawers, which provide invaluable storage space for an alarm clock, books, or other personal effects. The tatami can also be equipped with a complete set of shelves built under its base.

Tatamis are also ideal as single beds, since their ergonomic design is ideal for resting. It is a good idea to use a feather duvet with this type of bed.

1 The beds can be put together or separated according to individual needs.
2 Tatamis are also ideal as single beds.
3 The head of the bed is made up of sliding panels that reveal a fully equipped bookcase.

CLASSICAL AND FUNCTIONAL

Sofa design has evolved over the years, adapting itself to new fashions and experimenting with even the most daring and short-lived fads. Like any other classic, however, it possesses a core design that remains unchanged and never goes out of style. This apparent paradox describes the Metropolitan line: daring and innovative, yet also timeless and classical.

The Metropolitan is an extensive line of sectional sofas characterized by various angular designs. The collection includes a great variety of complements, which allow the sizes and shapes of the sofas to be adapted to any room, providing solutions for even the most difficult design problems.

The collection is, above all, conservative, and functional. Thanks to their soft, elegant contours, slightly rounded at the ends, Metropolitan sofas can fit into any type of decor, be it classical, innovative, or informal. They are also ideal for those who like to mix styles, since they can act as a bridge between the most diverse objects and furnishings.

The Metropolitan line of sofas has been carefully designed to ensure the highest degree of comfort and durability. The back, for example, rises to a three-quarter height in order to provide head support and allow maximum relaxation of the spine and lower back. The completely removable upholstery is made of high-

quality material made to withstand many years of use. The line consists of a sofa (available in four lengths) two chaises longues, a collection of modules, three hassocks, and three end-tables. The sofa legs are made of iron tubing coated with dull nickel plating or white lacquer. The legs are also available in beech.

The first photograph shows a Metropolitan sofa for three people. The large comfortable cushions on the seat and back of this elegant piece of furniture are only one of its many assets. The second photograph shows a long, sober arrangement of modules, and the third displays a large sofa coupled with a chaise longue at one end.

1 Metropolitan sofa for three.
2 An arrangement of various modules.
3 Sofa coupled with a chaise longue.

ATTENTION TO DETAIL

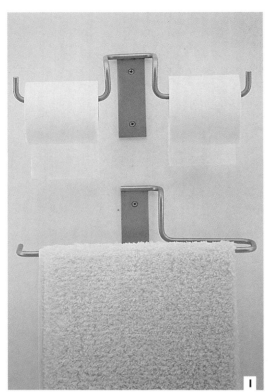

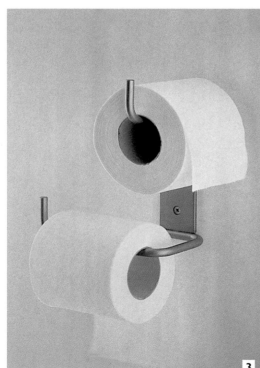

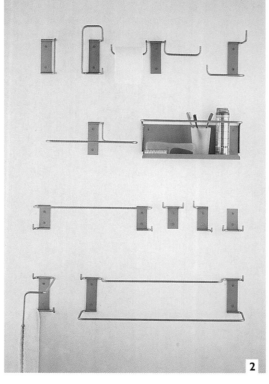

In a modern home even the smallest details should be carefully considered. As mundane and uninspiring as everyday objects may seem, they should be chosen with care and patience, since just one inappropriate detail can ruin the delicate balance of a room.

The items shown on the following pages all share a certain bare, industrial quality. Metallic structures and strong, minimalist contours are favored over bright colors and warm natural materials such as wood or cork. All of these pieces can be readily integrated into a modern home decorated in a fresh, youthful, and masculine style, lending a highly contemporary feel to the design.

One of the photographs shows a set of accessories, all reduced to a minimum: towel racks, trays, and glass holders. All are attached to the wall, although their attachments are invisible. While the accessories' bare, simple contours fit perfectly with any style of decor, they are best suited to stark, futuristic surroundings.

The third photograph shows an original toilet paper holder that holds two rolls. The key component of the holder is a metal plaque attached to the wall, from which two perpendicular metal rods emerge. These simple elements produce a surprising and attractive visual effect.

The last item is the Plac umbrella holder designed by Isabel Gamero Sicra and Jordi Escofet for BD Ediciones de Diseño. Made of satin-finish polished stainless steel and measuring 10 by 10 by 24 inches, its straight, well defined lines make it ideal for any modern home, as well as for offices seeking to have an up-to-date image.

1 Double toilet paper holder and towel rack, both from the E.T. collection.
2 Various bathroom components from the E.T. collection.
3 Double toilet paper holder with perpendicular arms.
4 The Plac umbrella holder: cold, minimalist elegance.

4

CLASSICAL SIMPLICITY

These photographs show several variations on the classic dining room table. Although each is different, they all spring from a common desire to re-interpret the characteristic appearance of this everyday piece of furniture while aiming for utmost esthetic simplicity.

The design that stands out most is the Sequoia table, with its firm, robust contours and broad legs. The large, solid-wood table-top rests perfectly balanced on two massive pieces of wood.

Versus, by the Italian designer Giacomo Passal, comes in a fixed and an extendable version. The table is made of maple wood that can be stained in various shades. Its convenient extension mechanism allows it to reach its full length simply by pulling on either of its sides.

The Via model by Matthew Hilton is surprising mainly for its great length. Its simple and un-adorned style is reminiscent of the tables found in old country houses.

Photograph 4 shows an elegant but youthful design by Giacomo Passal. The Balu design is available in fixed-length and extenda-ble versions, as well as with two different finishes: clear varnished cherry wood or maple stained in various colors. The legs come square or rounded. Like the Versus model described earlier, the extendable version is equip-ped with a simple and con-venient extension mechanism.

The last design discussed in this section is strikingly unique. Rondo, designed by Andreas Storiko, is a fascinating and attractive design whose appeal lies in the delicacy and refine-ment of its structure. The main axis is a round base from which perfectly tensed cables radiate upward until they reach a circu-lar pane of glass, giving the impression that the tabletop rests effortlessly and gracefully atop the crisscrossing cables.

1 Sequoia.
2 Versus.
3 Via.
4 Balu.
5 Rondo.

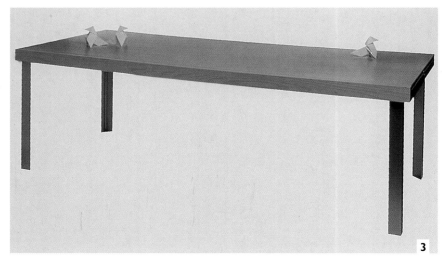

IMAGINATIVE LIGHTING

Lamps and lighting fixtures should be an integral part of a home's decorative scheme, whether they blend in discreetly or stand out proudly. In this section we present various models, some with traditional, conservative designs, and others whose innovative and daring forms make a statement in their own right.

Photographs 1 and 2 show the Brazos wall lamps designed by the team of Santa & Cole. The first design, Brazo Corto BC2, features a swiveling central trunk with a wooden handle at the end for adjusting the position of the lamp. The second photograph shows the Brazo Corto BC3, which is not adjustable.

The hanging Claris design, by the Spanish designer Lluís Porqueras, is made of pleated plastic and tinted glass, two materials that ensure excellent lighting.
Another elegant ceiling lamp is the Trèvol model by Massana-Tremoleda. The lamp's

 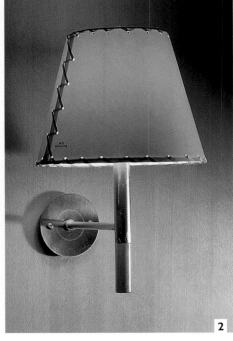

Moragas de Pie, by Antoni de Moragas, is ideal as a reading lamp, since its lampshade stays in the same position no matter how often the angle of the lamp is changed.

The Tripode G5 model by the team of Santa & Cole achieves a surprising effect with only a few simple components. An airy and seemingly fragile base supports a robust lampshade providing a remarkable amount of light. Finally, the Maija design, inspired by the shape of a beehive, is one of the most popular creations of Ilmari Tapiovaara, the Finnish master of postwar design.

design allows it to be attached to the ceiling at the electrical source or separated from it. It uses three light bulbs and features a translucent, polypropylene shade with a stainless steel structure and fittings.

Photographs 5 and 6 show the Steen model, by the late Steen Jorgensen. Jorgenson, a Danish designer who took up residence in Majorca, Spain, strove to lift the use of reflected light to its highest expression. His hanging lamp is exceptionally effective because of the careful placement of its slanted plates.

1 Brazo Corto BC2.
2 Brazo Corto BC3.
3 Claris.
4 Trèvol.
5 Steen.
6 Steen.
7 Moragas de Pie.
8 Tripode G5.
9 Maija series.

Children live in a world of their own, with their senses constantly developing. Sounds, shapes, colors, and light are food for this development. Therefore, the furniture that surrounds them should establish a special relationship with them a magical relationship that encourages participation.

The collection featured in this chapter was designed by Mathias Hoffman and offers a series of unique, charming, and imaginative components. All pieces are made of wicker, ideal for this type of room because it creates soft contours without dangerous edges. Sharp angles have been carefully replaced with rounded corners.

The first two photographs show different versions of the same model. A third variation can be found in photo-

graph 8. The piece is a version of the classic baby carriage. The central basket can rest on large wheels, like a wheelbarrow, or on its own curved base, like a rocking chair. As a rocking chair, two transverse rods with solid wooden balls at the ends act as counterweights and stops. Depending on the model, the top of the basket can hold a light canopy or rods with colorful geometric shapes.

For storing the baby's clothes, nothing is better than the wardrobe shown in the next figure, with its sliding wicker doors. The interior is lined with various shelves. One of the most striking aspects of its design is the elliptical contour of one of its sides.

Another original model is this practical crib, which can be turned into an attractive bench by the removal of one of its sides. It can stand on legs or a combination of legs and wheels. The sides are made of wicker and the base that holds the mattress is upholstered in bright blue material.

The final item is a unique highchair. Its sturdy, metal frame is completely covered with wicker, and the back can hold the same rods with geometric shapes that decorated the baby carriage mentioned earlier. The deep, half-moon-shaped drawer beneath the highchair is convenient for storing toys or other accessories.

1 Two transverse rods allow the carriage to be used as a rocker.

2 The baby carriage comes equipped with wheels and a cover.

3 An original children's wardrobe with sliding wicker doors.

4 This crib can be turned into a practical and attractive bench by removing one of its sides.

5 The completely assembled crib with wheels.

6 A charming wicker highchair. Decorative rods with geometric shapes can be attached to the back.

7 Detail shot of the basic version of the highchair.

8 The baby carriage with toys attached instead of the canopy.

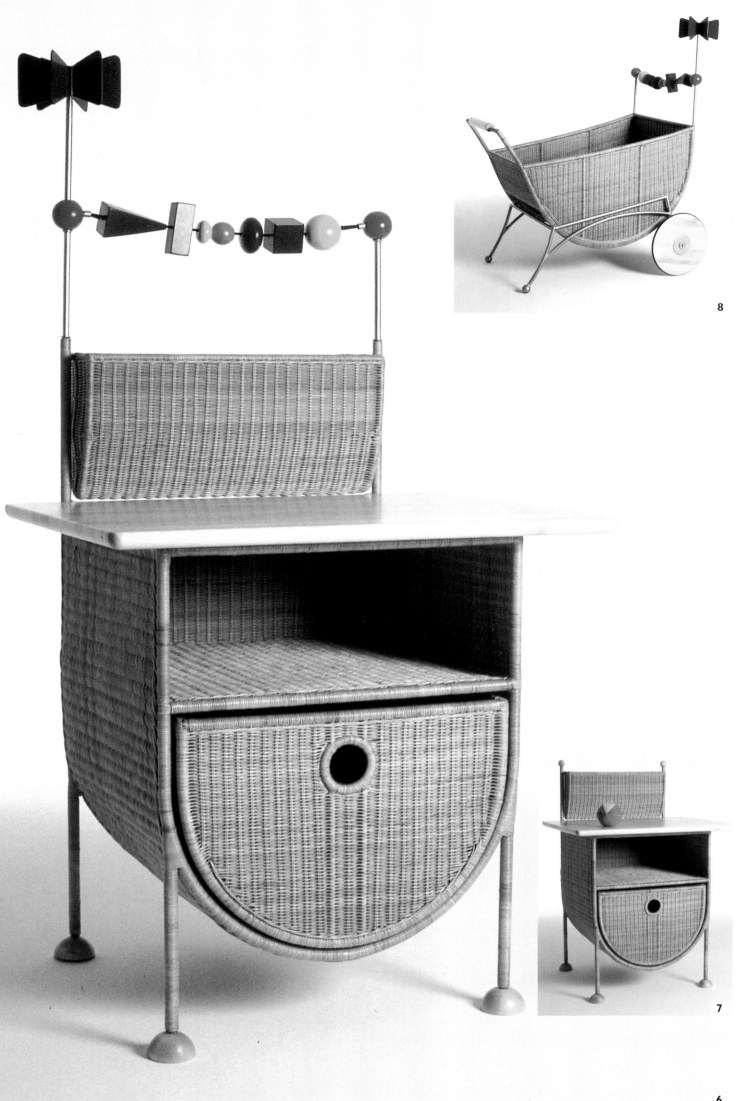

8

7

6

FURNITURE WITH CHARACTER

Dining room furniture should fulfill the underlying objective of creating a unique atmosphere, with each piece playing a role in the arrangement as a whole. The items here all share a common look. They are simple, with nearly bare contours, and clean, smooth surfaces.

The table and sideboard shown in the first photograph are from the Tama collection by Antoni Riera. The table features a metal structure supporting the wooden tabletop. The design strives for a unified effect by using only two planes. The sideboard is actually no more than a container based on a metallic structure. Both pieces offer an exterior look that is extremely simple, and that is based completely on right angles, smooth surfaces, and a complete absence of superfluous ornaments.

Teorema, designed by Paco Carrús for the Forum collection, is a set of furniture that can turn any corner of the house into a work space. The set is composed of two pieces, a solid but graceful desk and a small chest of drawers that is also available as a filing cabinet.

The Nayra coffee table by Antoni Riera consists of parallel planes placed on top of one another. The lower surface is made of cherry or maple veneer with a smaller sheet of plate glass suspended over it.

Finally, the Nayra dressing table, also designed by Antoni Riera, is a streamlined piece based on clean, straight lines and right angles. Its only decorative elements are the drawer handles placed repetitively between the horizontal lines formed by the drawers. At the top, a door swings down to reveal a mirror and three small drawers.

1 Dining room table and sideboard from the Tama collection.
2 Teorema desk and filing cabinet, from the Forum collection.
3 Coffee table from the Nayra collection.
4 Dressing table from the Nayra collection.

3

GOOD SEATS

A design for any kind of seat, a chair, stool or armchair, can never be based only on fashion and appearance. No matter how attractive or innovative a chair is, it is useless if it is uncomfortable. The designs featured here have all succeeded in maintaining a perfect balance between function and appearance.

The first photograph shows different versions of the Party model designed by Gabriel Teixidó for Grassoler. The chair features a solid wooden structure padded with polyester, with suspension provided by elastic cinches. The seat is made of 77-pound, resilient polyester covered with acrylic material. The back and arms are also covered with acrylic and padded with polyester, in this case with a resilience of 75 pounds. The streamlined legs are made of varnished beech and are available in the following tones: natural, walnut, cherry, mahogany, or black lacquer. Other options are chrome legs and wheels, as well as removable upholstery.

Also designed by Gabriel Teixidó for Grassoler, the Sunset sofa and armchair are made of polyester padding on a solid wooden frame. The seat suspension is based on a set of springs, and the back is reinforced with elastic cinches and filled with a blend of polyester and feathers. The legs, hidden behind the flaps of the upholstery, are made of varnished beech and are available in several tones: natural, walnut, cherry, or black lacquer. The upholstery on this model is completely removable.

Another of Gabriel Teixidó's designs for Grassoler is the Parcel armchair in the third photograph. This chair features comfortable, rounded contours and a solid wooden structure padded with polyester. Elastic cinches provide suspension, and the back and arms are padded with highly resilient polyester. The varnished beech legs are available in natural, walnut, or cherry tones, as well as black lacquer. The chair is also available with removable upholstery.

Finally, the Flower model, designed by Giulano Cappelletti and Enzo Pozzoli for Grassoler, is inspired by the elegance of the classic Chester sofas. Its structure is made of painted iron and epoxy, and its suspension is based on modular system of springs. The upholstery on this model is completely removable.

1 Three versions of the Party model of chairs.
2 The Sunset sofa and armchair.
3 The Parcel armchair is characterized by its soft, rounded contours.
4 The Flower model: a classic brought up to date.

4

EVERYDAY OBJECTS

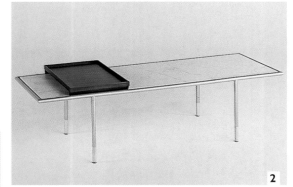

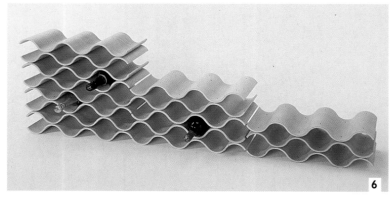

Design is an important aspect of even the humblest and most commonplace household objects. Without disregarding their function, simple objects can take on new shapes that are often surprisingly different from those customarily seen. Although not apparent at first glance, much hard work and imagination lie behind these designs.

Although the objects featured in this section are all quite different from one another in terms of their household function, they all have one thing in common, their unique and original design.

The three tables that begin this chapter are surprising in their simplicity. The first is the Goa model, designed by Didier Gómez. This table is composed of two thin sheets placed one over the other. Anna Bianca by Christophe Pillet is an even simpler design, eliminating one of the sheets. The slanted legs of the third design, Magic Table, by the Atelier EOOS firm, are reminiscent of the practical simplicity of the picnic table.

Several items provide imaginative solutions for storage. The Espiral coat hangers by M. Ferrer and R. Blanco, the Monolit hanger by Eduardo Fernández, and the Teula/Wave bottle rack by Ines & Milà are all examples of how innovation can be applied to everyday objects. Espiral uses seemingly random twists and turns, whereas Monolit is based on straight, sober lines. Teula/Wave, on the other hand, takes its inspiration from the undulating lines of shingles.

Many items displayed in this section are inventive variations on common household objects. The 10 line chair by Pascal Mourgue sports a firm but streamlined look. Two shelving designs taking a minimalist approach to wall storage are Inclit by Mariano Ferrer, and Shed, by Design & Design. The Frank metal telephone rack is similarly minimalist, and is available in a variety of colors.

Finally, the Capicúa line, by Sergi and Oscar Devesa, is a collection of tables. The concept underlying this collection relies on the use of a cast aluminum foot that can be inverted or combined with other, identical pieces to make a support for the tabletop. This ingenious system permits several different combinations.

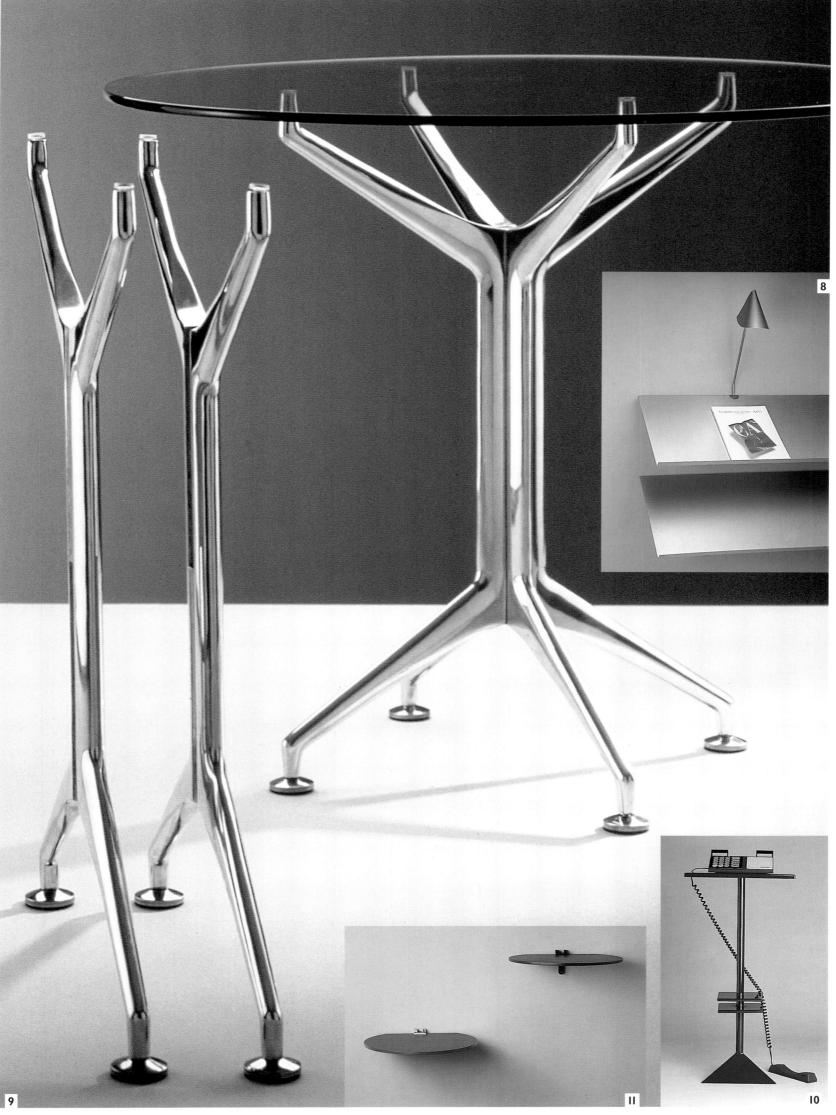

AMAZING GRACE

Although simple, stools can possess a graceful, streamlined elegance. Not long ago they were rarely found in homes, and the few that were in homes were often rustic and unattractive. Fortunately, contemporary interior design principles have eliminated those stereotypes and the classic barstool has begun to reappear in many family homes.

Stools are often the best example of design simplicity, since very few objects obtain such satisfactory results from so few components. The first selection is Nuta, three attractive stools designed by Lluís Pau. These three stools feature a metal structure in different heights (18, 24, and 30 inches) and two types of seats, wooden or chrome. A metal ring fastens around the three legs, strengthening the structure and allowing it to serve as a foot rest. The graceful simplicity and strength of this design make these stools equally suited to homes or establishments such as bars or restaurants. Their clean, unadorned beauty makes them a decorative addition to any kitchen or bathroom.

The Charly stools are similar in design to the Nuta model. Their structure is also made of metal, although the bars used are thicker,

giving them even greater stability and strength. The seat is made of wood, but is also available in other material and colors. The metal ring connects the legs around the inside edge.

The last selection is the Comedia model by V. Gallego. This 30-inch-high stool features an exceptional, eye-catching design. Two identical legs are combined with another to create an unusual tripod supporting a cushioned seat upholstered with cloth in various colors. The two equal legs stand almost straight up, while the third juts out. This odd leg holds a bar that acts as a foot rest. The metal parts are available in chrome or painted in two colors, textured black or metallic aluminum.

1 Nuta stools.
2 Charly stools.
3 Comedia stools.

3

RELAXING ENVIRONMENTS

1 "Nocto comes equipped with hanging
   bookcases that slide along aluminum rails.

2 The collection is a stunning example
   of logic and function.

3 Reading lamps can be attached to the
   top of the panel.

4 The panel disappears behind a shelf that
   juts out for use as a night table.

The interior design of bedrooms should strive to promote rest and relaxation, and should emphasize balance above all. Interruptions or excesses in decor can be irritating or overwhelming. Therefore, the decorator should strive for simplicity, since bedrooms with only a few functional pieces are generally more comforting and relaxing.

The Nocto collection by Team Form Ag is a prime example of that principle, with its capacity to create light, well-balanced combinations. Nocto consists of a large, rectangular panel placed behind the bed, and incorporates several elements: a headboard, night tables, and a bookcase.

The visual airiness of the Nocto collection comes from its unique design. The panel seems to float magically in midair, disappearing behind a shelf that juts out for use as a night table.

The panels are dotted with aluminum fittings that hold bookcases of various sizes. Nocto is also available with translucent plastic drawers that fit into the open sections of the hanging bookcases. One of the design's most useful features is that the components slide along the aluminum rails so that the arrangement can be easily changed.

The panels come in lengths ranging from 52 to 92 inches. This makes it possible to combine them with many sizes of beds, ranging from 35 to 79 inches wide. A large, upholstered cushion may also be incorporated at the head of the bed. Along with large pillows and optional reading lamps, this makes a perfect arrangement for reading comfortably in bed. Nocto is available in the following finishes: light gray lacquer, clear white lacquer, champagne lacquer, natural maple, and light maple.

The timeless elegance of its design, coupled with its peerless practicality make Nocto an exceptional collection whose discreet beauty will probably remain undiminished for years to come.

PLASTIC AND METAL

Plastic and metal make a perfect team, and are a part of many of today's design schemes. Metal, no matter what kind it may be, brings solidity to any object, while plastic adds an informal touch. It is worth mentioning that plastic is no longer the tacky, low-quality material of the past. Nowadays, there is a great variety of high-quality plastics that are beautiful and perfectly finished.

The chairs shown were designed by the noted Milanese designer Carlo Bartoli. To give an idea of Bartoli's importance in the world of design, two of his creations form part of the permanent collections of prestigious museums. The Gaia armchair is on display at the New York Museum of Modern Art, while the Sophia chair is exhibited at the Lubania Museum of Architecture.

Bartoli defines his projects as "the point where technology meets inspiration," and the Breeze chair is a clear example of this philosophy. For this piece, Bartoli took advantage of knowledge about the treatment of metal and applied it to modern design. Breeze is a functional and tasteful model that has a sophisticated balance of shapes. This balance is most evident in the armrests, which are attached directly to the legs. This chair is part of a collection that includes tables and barstools. It has an aluminum structure which supports a recyclable polypropylene body. It measures 57 by 48 by 79 centimeters (22 by 19 by 31 inches). An upholstered version is also available. In 1997 this model became part of the permanent exhibition at the Thessalonian Museum of Design.

The Storm chair is available with or without arms. It features a steel structure that can be chromed or varnished, and its body is made of recyclable polypropylene. This model is characterized by its streamlined and reserved contours and its svelte, well-balanced shapes. The armrests, which rise boldly from the rear part of the back, are available covered with protective plastic. Storm is available in several colors, including cream, pink, lavender, white, green, black, blue and gray. Its accessories include a round table and a basket for holding personal effects.

1

2

3

14

4

5

1 The Breeze chair is ideal for offices.
2 The Breeze chair with a blue finish.
3 The Breeze chair features
   a one-piece structure.
4 The Breeze chair can also be used
   for exterior decoration.
5 The Storm chair.

SOFAS FOR ANY NEED

Many collections of sofas on the market consist of modules that can be interchanged as needed. Sofas designed in this way are often just as practical as those made to order, although less expensive. Nevertheless, many people prefer unique and indivisible pieces of furniture, that can often be classic pieces of interior design.

The models featured here were all created by the Italian designer Antonio Citterio, who specializes in clean lines and simple shapes.

The first collection, called Charles, is made up of fourteen pieces which can be combined to create various arrangements. In this way, a sofa can fit perfectly even in a room with unusual angles and corners. These sofas are built around a structure of pressure-cast aluminum, with legs made of the same material. The base of the sofa is completely upholstered and connected to the armrests, giving a the piece a feeling of continuity. Large, firm cushions cover the seats, with soft cushions resting on top. The collection includes modules to fulfill a variety of needs: sofas of various sizes, corner pieces to use as connections, and chaises longues, among others.

The Dandy collection is characterized by modern contours, and includes various sizes of sofas, an armchair, and a charming hassock. These pieces are discreetly elegant, making them ideal for any household. Their soft, rounded corners give them an innocent charm that fits especially well with a youthful or informal style of decoration. The bare, slightly slanted back is one of the most attractive features of the collection. The soft seat cushions, which can be supplemented by other cushions, add a touch of comfortable frivolity to the collection. The legs are available in flat nickel-coated steel, or covered with transparent plastic or cherry veneer.

1 Arrangement of modules from the Charles collection, with two sofas connected at the middle.
2 Charles sofa with armrests connected to a chaise longue also from the Charles collection.
3 Two armchairs from the Dandy collection.
4 Charles sofa without armrests connected to a chaise longue also from the Charles collection.

IMPECCABLE DESIGN

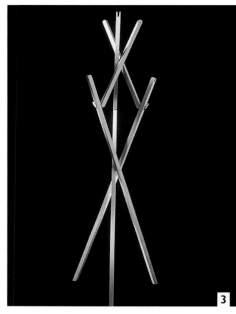

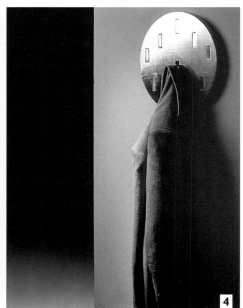

All of the accessories shown here fulfill practical needs while also striving for utmost simplicity.

The first model is the Tria bookshelf designed by Massana-Tremoleda. The module is composed of ladder-shaped vertical supports that hold metal or wooden shelves. The wide selection of components (two depths, two widths, and three lengths) allows the module to adapt to any location.

The next model, Primavesi, is a container inspired by the legendary piece designed by J. Hoffmann in turn-of-the-century Vienna. The plant and umbrella holders, designed by Gabriel Mora and Santiago Roqueta in 1975, were a humble tribute to Hoffmann's enormous contributions to modern design.

The two coat racks, Hut AB by Konstantin Grcic and Perchalum by Felo Baixauli, are fine examples of how practicality and beauty can be brought together in one piece of furniture. Hut AB is made of six waxed ash wood bars connected by sliding rails. At the end of each rail is an anodized aluminum hook for hanging clothes. When not being used, Hut AB can be folded to take up less space. The hangers on the Perchalum model, which is made of aluminum, can also be folded up when not in use.

Another original design is the Summa table, designed by Jon Gasca. This practical piece is composed of a folding chair with a canvas seat which can be transformed into a table by placing a round tray on top. The model is made of wood and aluminum, with details in cherry and beech.

The Gira lamp, by J. M. Massana, J. M. Tremoleda, and M. Ferrer, has undergone a profound transformation since its introduction in 1978. The original model featured an artificial stone base. The new version, Gira Mini, has gone back to the basics with the use of natural marble.

Finally, the Riga collection of accessories, by Massana-Tremoleda, consists of an ashtray and two wastepaper baskets. In addition to their stunning design, these accessories are notable for their durability and ease of maintenance. The ashtray's receptacle is made of anodized aluminum, and the wastepaper baskets feature interior supports for holding plastic garbage bags.

1 Tria shelves.
2 Primavesi plant and umbrella holders.
3 Hut AB coat rack.
4 Perchalum coat rack.
5 Summa table.
6 Gira lamp with marble base.
7 Riga collection of accessories.

6

7

MAKING ROOM

The storage of household objects is an increasingly important problem in homes, and in particular for apartments. Making the best use of space is essential. Closets and wardrobes are helpful in creating storage space in any type of home. The latest designs feature more storage space on the inside while taking up less visual space on the outside compared to older, bulkier models. The collection dealt with here, Atlante, by Studio Kairos, is an excellent example.

The first characteristic noticeable in these photographs is the unquestionable elegance of the collection. When closed, the closets form a fundamental part of the decor, adding a subdued touch of personality to the room. Once opened, they reveal a surprisingly spacious interior, divided into logical, well organized compartments. Large sliding panels, available in wood or in acid-treated glass, provide easy access to the interior. The panels are attached to rails at the top, and slide smoothly and silently on invisible wheels. Both panels can be moved in two directions and slide on top of each other to allow access to every corner of the interior.

The closets are fully equipped and employ a practical system of vertical aluminum supports instead of more traditional fixed dividing panels. The supports can hold a variety of shelves, drawers, and rods, combinable and arrangeable according to personal needs. Because of the flexibility of this system, personal effects can be conveniently organized, as in the adage "a place for everything and everything in its place."

The Atlante collection can also be used to make walk-in closets. The result is a virtual room, with a practically unlimited number of configurations for storage. The walls of Atlante walk-in closets are covered with a grid of horizontal and vertical bars supporting shelves and other components. The lower part of the walls holds easily moved containers and modules. The components are available in white plastic, natural cherry, or wengé.

2

I

1 The Atlante collection features a large variety of components for organizing personal effects.

2 Interior of a walk-in closet.

3 The sliding panels can be moved in both directions.

LIGHT AS A FEATHER

Contemporary interior design tends to avoid extremes. It favors lightness and simplicity over bulk and ornamentation. For this reason, many manufacturers are turning to plant fiber or are producing furniture with surprisingly minimalist designs and a streamlined, almost ethereal, look. Pieces designed with this in mind have a restrained quality that is attractive without seeming overwhelming.

The Uragano chair featured in the first photograph was designed by Vico Magistretti. This chair features a subtly classical design with a contemporary touch. It is perfect for both indoor and outdoor use and features a wooden frame painted in a soft violet color. The seat and back are of delicately woven wicker, which produces a strikingly beautiful effect. The curved back provides comfortable back support.

The second and third photographs feature the Frog sofa by Piero Lissoni in different versions. This clean-lined, minimalist piece exudes a youthful and graceful sense. Cushions can be added to make this beautifully designed sofa more comfortable. This model has a metal frame coated with epoxy paint in white, black, or aluminum gray. The frame is covered with a handmade net of durable leather, which can be replaced by a net of black or white cotton straps. The collection also includes a version with cushions upholstered in leather or cloth, as well as a three-seater model and a bench. The collection is completed by an outdoor version with a stainless steel frame and upholstery in PVC.

The last photograph shows three chairs with a crisp, original design. These chairs are three different versions of the Chair de Gervason, which has a wooden structure covered with interwoven strips of plant fiber. These models are characterized by their strong, straight lines and simple elegance. The low chair is available with or without armrests, and the most streamlined model features an especially long back.

1

1 The Uragano chair.
2 The three-seater version of the Frog sofa.
3 Two elegant chairs from the Frog line.
4 Three versions of the Chair de Gervason.

2

ELEGANT COLLECTIONS

The pieces of furniture presented here all belong to complete collections which can provide furnishing and decor for an entire house. These modern lines of furniture all feature a wide variety of components and modules that can be readily adapted to any room. Carefully planned and imaginative use of the components result in a unique style of interior that also fulfills specific functional needs.

The first photograph shows an arrangement from the Domus line by Antonio Citterio. The key piece is the spacious bookcase made up of four vertical modules and five horizontal spaces. A sliding panel can be moved up or down, and features several cabinet shelves inside. The vertical modules can be arranged in various configurations, and are available in natural or varnished wood, as well as glass. As a result of this variety of arrangements and materials, the appearance of the bookcase can vary dramatically.

The Apta collection, also by Antonio Citterio, is guaranteed to lend elegance to any dining room. The table, characterized by clean, simple lines, is composed of three panels. The two smaller panels, connected by a metal bar, act as supports, while the third forms the tabletop. This ample table can hold up to ten people. The armless chairs feature a well padded seat, streamlined, sturdy legs, and a low back.

The last item featured in this section is an elegant buffet from the Apta collection. The body of the buffet is a long piece with six drawers, supported by slender, sturdy metal legs. The structure of the buffet is made of nickel-plated steel with a satin finish, and the body is available in light oak or wengé. The classical but timeless design of this model makes it a piece of furniture that will never go out of style.

All of the pieces of furniture in this section have the rare quality of creating a unique atmosphere in the rooms that contain them. They establish a harmonious relationship with the surrounding furniture, no matter what the style. This quality is complemented by their practical and functional design.

1 Bookcase from the Domus line.
2 Table and chairs from the Apta collection.
3 Buffet from the Apta collection.

2

3

UNIQUE SPACES

Some pieces of furniture create a sense of peace and beauty in a room. They carry an aura of serene elegance, which is the antithesis of eccentricity. These pieces are the epitome of discretion, they never stand out, but rather, they let themselves be noticed with an air of calculated indifference.

The pieces chosen for this section are privileged members of this exquisite group. Their design balances practical and esthetic considerations and has the quiet visual force to make them into classics.

The first photograph shows two display cabinets from the Apta collection by the Italian artist Antonio Citterio. This collection includes furniture for living rooms and dining rooms, such as chairs, armchairs, tables, and buffets, as well as for bedroom furniture, including beds, night tables, wardrobes, and dressing tables. The cabinets shown here are made of stripped oak, although they are also available in wengé. They have enough compartments to organize all the accessories needed for the table. The upper part of the cabinets has two shelves and features two glass doors that slide up and down. The lower doors are hinged, and enclose a drawer and more shelves.

The bookcase in the second photograph belongs to the Domus line, also by Citterio. This is a modular collection that can be arranged in various configurations. This photograph shows the Glass Flag, one of the most original elements of the series. The Glass Flag is a pane of translucent glass that partially or totally protects the bookcase. The flag-shaped pane of glass rotates around a metal pole.

The model shown in the third photograph is also from the Domus line. It features two horizontal doors that slide up and down.

Finally, the Harry sofa in photograph 4 is a modular piece with soft padded seats and a sturdy, modern appearance. The series includes sofas in three lengths, an armchair, and various additional modules, such as right and left end-pieces, a central piece without arms, a corner module, and a chaise longue.

1 *Display cabinets from the "Apta" collection.*
2 *Bookcase from the Domus line, with its unique Glass Flag.*
3 *Bookcase from the Domus line with horizontal sliding doors.*
4 *Harry sofa.*

A GOOD NIGHT'S SLEEP

A bed should be chosen with care, since approximately one third of our life is spent sleeping. Fortunately, there are many models to choose from which are both anatomically designed and esthetically pleasing. Three of these designs are featured here.

All models in this section are remarkable for their elegance, beauty, and harmony. They all show the modern tendency of eschewing superfluous ornamentation in favor of utmost simplicity, and are all based on simple structures inspired by pure forms and clean lines. Their legs are nearly invisible or replaced by wheels, and they all lack canopies or ostentatious headboards.

The first design shown is the Pilgrim model by Vico Magistretti. Pilgrim is a double bed which rests on metal legs or wheels with brakes. The bed features a beech base with elegantly upholstered borders. The most distinctive characteristic of the Pilgrim model is its wide headboard consisting of a metal structure padded with a thick layer of polyurethane foam. The headboard leans slightly backward, bringing a dynamic sense to the design. Like the rest of the bed, it features removable upholstery.

Ribbon, another design by Vico Magistretti, also owes its sense of originality to its unique headboard, which is made of a 2-inch thick beech board attached to the wall by cotton strips. This model is ideal for a youthful or exotic atmosphere, since it neatly combines colonial and minimalist design. The headboard features completely removable upholstery for easy cleaning.

Peter Maly Bett is an especially subdued and streamlined design. Its main component is its wide upholstered base. The base is sturdy and firm, and lacks any lateral protection or decoration. The headboard consists of two large upholstered squares.

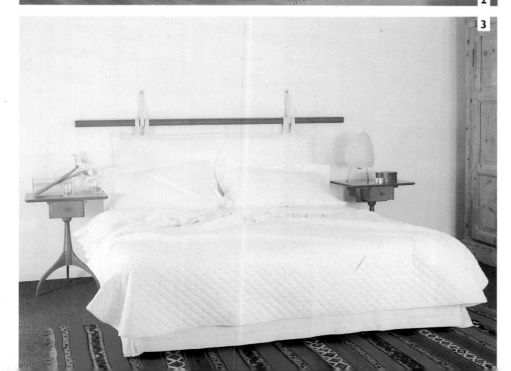

1 The Pilgrim.
2 The Pilgrim is available with wheels or metal legs.
3 The Ribbon.
4 The Peter Maly Bett.

WARM AND INVITING NOOKS

Any corner of the house can become a cozy place to spend a relaxing moment on a rainy day. The only things necessary are a few essential pieces that bring their own special character to the space. The use of distinct colors or textures also help distinguish the area from its surroundings and give it personality. Shown here is a line of chairs that serve as essential furnishings, as well as a practical reading lamp.

The first and third photographs show rooms that are prime examples of interiors that are designed to be warm, personal, distinguished, and discreet. All elements have been carefully chosen and kept to a minimum to avoid crowding the space. The Betibó chairs, created by the Spanish designer Carlos Tíscarin in 1996, are an essential part of the decor. These comfortable pieces are at once modern and elegant.

The Betibó model is streamlined and functional. Its design is based on a judicious combination of straight and curved lines. Straight lines are used for the front legs and seat, while curved lines dominate the rear legs and back, which are joined in one piece, as well as the armrests. This model can be ordered with or without armrests, and is available in three versions. There is a washable version with a choice of either slipcover or a naturally finished pith wickerwork, both of which are completely removeable. A full selection of cushioned materials can be chosen instead for upholstery. A third option is naturally finished pith woven directly onto the structure. The structure is made of solid beech, which can be lacquered in different colors.

The second photograph displays a practical device for reading: the Hi-Fi lamp, designed by Gabriel Teixidó in 1997. Hi-Fi is a modern version of the classic adjustable reading lamp that used a clamp instead of a base, with the lampshade attached directly to the light bulb by means of another clamp. The Hi-Fi model also uses a clamp system, but its design is much more simple and streamlined. The lamp features an on/off switch and uses halogen bulbs. The lampshade can be swiveled 360 degrees, making it comfortable to use. Its three-yard-long cord allows it to be placed in any location, and the clamp adjusts to surfaces up to 1.4 inches wide. It uses two 20-watt bulbs and features a flat chrome finish.

1 The Betibó chairs can fit with any type of decor.
2 The Hi-Fi reading lamp.
3 The Betibó chairs are available with or without armrests.

TIMELESS BEAUTY

1 *The Duo line combines esthetics and function.*
2 *The collection allows an almost infinite number of possible compositions.*
3 *The panes of translucent glass bring a light airy touch to the bookcase.*

The success or failure of a design depends not only on its elegant and attractive appearance, but also on its function. Although a piece of furniture may have beautiful contours and an attractive silhouette, it will soon be forgotten if it is uncomfortable and illogically designed. On the other hand, designs that perform the difficult feat of balancing these two factors have a good chance of enduring as classics. Such is undoubtedly the case for the Duo collection featured on the following pages.

The main characteristics of this collection by Peter Maly are its simplicity and clean lines. The Duo collection is a line of shelves and storage units designed to provide a variety of possible combinations. The pieces are remarkable for their classical and timeless design, as well as for their robust and durable construction. Furniture arrangements built with this collection imbue a room with peace and relaxation, creating a welcome refuge from the hectic world. The storage units have ample space and can be easily stacked or moved.

In the 1980s, the Duo line became a modern classic; a point of reference imitated and adapted by designers all over the world. Always faithful to an underlying principle of simplicity, Maly managed to create a new esthetic by taking advantage of new possibilities offered by modern materials. Duo is available in several finishes and materials, such as beech, black or gray lacquer, or glass, so that each person is free to create a unique version.

In the first photograph, Duo is used as a bookcase as part of a living room. The bookcase is made up of two closed modules, one on each side, and a spacious, open storage space in the center. The central space is composed of various compartments for storing a variety of objects.

The second photograph shows an informal, combined living and dining room. Here the bookcase stretches nearly from wall to wall and is based around three narrow upright cabinets with shelves between. One of the gaps in the module holds a chest of drawers, while the other may hold a television.

The third composition is a square module divided into several compartments. Several of the compartments hold drawers, and the entire piece may be enclosed by means of translucent panes of glass.

1

2

ESSENTIAL ACCESSORIES

The furniture of any house includes certain pieces without which everyday life would be difficult, if not impossible. However, many other pieces help make a home more comfortable, convenient, and appealing, even though they may not be as essential. The designs featured here fall into this second category.

Photographs 2 and 4 display an exceptional design called Glassbox, created by Jorge Pensi in 1996. This design won the Silver Delta Award in the 1996 edition of the ADI-FAD. Glassbox is, as its name suggests, a glass case with a slender wooden frame. Various components of the series can be combined to produce any number of pieces, from a simple box to a vertical display case, a coffee table, or a hanging china closet. These pieces fit easily into any room of the house, living room, bathroom, kitchen, or bedroom.

The second photograph shows a coffee table from the series. The tabletop is actually a hinged door that swings up. A streamlined vertical display case is featured in photograph 4. The case is composed of several Glassbox containers stacked one atop the other. These containers are excellent for protecting small objects from dust.

If originality is the prime consideration, the Picnic coffee table by Paco Martínez is an imaginative and practical choice. Because of its two foldable tabletops (connected at the center), the Picnic table can be used to store all objects that need to be kept at arm's reach in a living room, such as books, magazines, or compact discs. A handsome and delicate weave of cherry wood leaves the contents partly visible, highlighting the practical side of the piece. At the same time, the pattern gives the table an unmistakable personality, suggestive of a traditional picnic basket. Its circular shape and built-in wheels make the table easy to place in any part of the room.

Photograph 3 displays a modern version of the classic pedestal table. Its circular tabletop rests on a single leg that divides into four feet at ground level. This design gives the table a light and streamlined look without sacrificing firm support. Pedestal tables are currently very popular because they can be used as a coffee table, corner table, or telephone table.

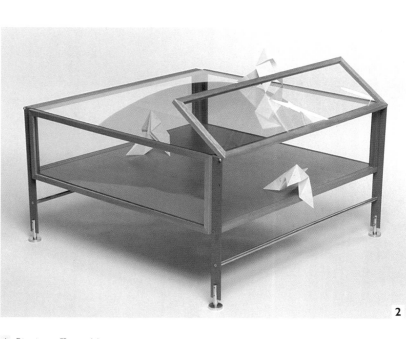

1 Picnic coffee table.
2 Glassbox coffee table.
3 A classic pedestal table.
4 Glassbox display case.

MAKE YOURSELF AT HOME

Certain rooms seem to have been especially well designed to be inhabited. These rooms have an air of warmth and familiarity about them; they seem to invite us in and to tell us to pull up a chair and relax. Such an atmosphere is rarely the product of chance. It results from a careful choice of every detail in the room, from the main pieces of furniture to the smallest accessories. When all of these aspects join harmoniously, the outcome is a triumph of interior design.

The rooms shown in the first and fourth photographs were decorated with the Duo collection by Peter Maly. This collection is remarkable for its tireless, classic appearance and the calm and relaxing balance of its design, which is at once handsome and practical. The components can be combined to produce a plethora of compositions. Shown here is a bookcase made up of three slender cabinets in lacquered aluminum connected by various horizontal shelves and cabinets in natural beech. The low buffet with drawers that holds the television and videocassette player is also from the Duo collection. The Duo line makes an ideal substitute for the traditional bookcase, which often looks too bulky when placed in small rooms.

The Trinus model in photograph 2 is an eye-catching design by Jonas Kressel and Ivo Schelle. It rests on wheels, so that it can be easily moved to any part of the room. This surprisingly simple design can be transformed effortlessly from a stylish armchair or sofa into a comfortable bed. The Trinus model can also be used as a chaise longue, and its clean, simple design allows it to blend into any style of decor.

For those who want to add a touch of originality to their living room, the Forum 322 sofa by Anita Schmidt is the ideal choice. It comes upholstered in blue leather as well as red or striped material. Its graceful, streamlined contours make it an example of harmonious design, while the thick, soft padding contrasts with the cold simplicity of the metal legs. The Forum 322 sofa is a strikingly beautiful combination of straight and curved lines whose perfectly balanced angles create a stunning effect.

1 The Duo collection is an ideal substitute for the classic bookcase.
2 The Trinus sofa bed.
3 The Forum 322 sofa.
4 An elegant arrangement from the Duo collection.

MODULAR CONSTRUCTION

Modular designs have nowadays almost completely replaced the traditional one-piece bookcase. Although they possess a certain charm, the one-piece models tend to take up an excessive amount of space and rarely fit snugly into a room. The usual result was wasted space at either end of the piece of furniture, making the room more difficult to organize. The models featured on the following pages are ideal solutions for this kind of problem. Their modular design allows anyone to construct an attractive bookcase that fits tightly from wall to wall, without wasting an inch of precious space.

The first collection featured in this chapter is Natura, displayed in photographs 1, 2, and 3. This collection was designed by Dieter Reinhold and Siegfried Bensinger. The basic pieces come in a maximum height of 256 centimeters (8 feet, 5 inches), although taller models are also available in increments of 20 centimeters (8 inches). The collection also includes special modules, which constitute small bookcases with several shelves. These pieces are available in widths of 120, 180, or 240 centimeters (47, 71, or 94 inches). The closed modules are available with three kinds of doors: sliding, folding, or hinged. The surface can be smooth or grainy.

Natura is available in several materials, such as glass, maple, or lacquer. These materials can be combined in surprising ways. For example, the delicate glass shelves gleam against the aquamarine lacquer of the maple modules featured in photograph 3. The top panel, forming a kind of ceiling for the bookcase, can hold built-in spotlights with protection to avoid glare.

The fourth photograph presents a room decorated with pieces from the Berlin collection. The unit that covers the wall is made of natural colored cherry wood and is outstanding because of its balanced composition. The spaces and modules are logically distributed for optimal use, combining shelves and gaps of various sizes. The central module features hinged glass doors, as if it were an independent display case. Another unique feature is the table for the television and videocassette player, which can be easily moved because of its built-in wheels.

1   A module from the Natura collection, which holds the television and videocassette player.
2   A wall-to-wall bookcase built with the Natura collection.
3   This Natura bookcase does not reach the ceiling. Portholes have been placed in the upper panel.
4   A composition from the Berlin collection.

64

4

SUBTLE ELEGANCE

1

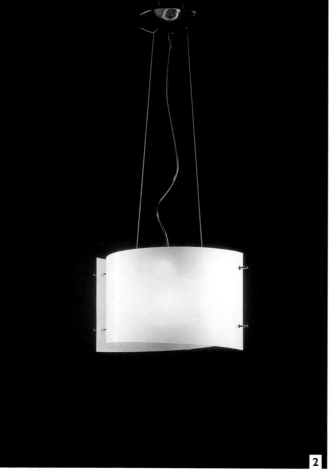

2

Choosing a ceiling lamp is not a matter that should be taken lightly, since a rash choice can ruin even the best decorative schemes. The main thing to keep in mind is that this kind of lamp should never be gaudy or extravagant, but rather discreet and unobtrusive, except in the unlikely case that it is decorating a baroque palace. The models featured here are ideal for bringing warmth and light into any tastefully decorated home, thanks to their subtle designs.

The first photograph shows the Alvar model, designed by J. M. Magem. This simple hanging lamp is striking for the abundant and unusual light it produces. The light escapes through the gaps in its three volumes to produce an exceptionally clear and pure effect. Its aluminum structure is available in anodized or white finishes, and it uses standard light bulbs.

The Doble model, also designed by J. M. Magem, belongs to an entire collection of lamps that includes floor, table, and ceiling models. Its clean, simple contours give it a unique elegance that allows it to fit in with a wide range of decorative styles. Its metal structure comes in a chromed finish, while its base is covered with textured paint. The shade is composed of two pieces of curved glass which have been engraved and tinted. This model also uses standard light bulbs.

Finally, the Plisada model is a hanging lamp designed by J. M. Magem. This lamp hangs from the ceiling on steel cables with a counterbalance that allows the height to be adjusted. Magem's design combines the classicism of its traditional lampshade, made of pleated cloth, with the practicality afforded by the adjustable mechanism. Plisada is a prime example of how a classic design can be brought up to date and adapted to modern needs.

All of these models complement the rest of the furniture and become part of the whole decorative scheme. They are indispensable elements which can bring personality and character to a room.

3

Coffee tables, end tables, and other small, auxiliary tables are attractive and practical pieces that give a room the finishing touch that is essential to any interior design scheme. They can occupy difficult corners and fulfill simple but often essential needs, such as providing a place to put snacks, lamps, or telephones. The three models featured on these pages are outstanding for their original, practical, and clean design.

The table in the first paragraph is the P-021 model by M. C. Mobles. It is a rectangular table made of beech. Its four hinged doors provide access to the inside of the table, which can be used as a handy storage space. Both the tabletop and the doors are made of glass that has a sandy finish. Straight lines predominate in the design, especially in the body of the table, which is completely rectangular. The legs, however, are slightly curved, offering an attractive counterpoint to the rest of the design. Delicate serigraphy on the lateral glass doors brings a personal touch to this elegant piece of furniture, which measures 16 by 39 by 39 inches.

The Hop-Hop model is remarkable for its stark simplicity. Raising the hinged tabletop reveals a surprisingly well equipped interior that can be used for storage. The table measures 43 by 24 inches.

The S-163 model is available as a coffee table or a corner table. Both are circular in shape and stand on cone-shaped legs. The most characteristic features of the model are the two parallel tabletops, which sit one atop the other and are connected by metal rods. The corner table has a lighter and more slender design. It stands on three streamlined legs and measures 22 inches by 16 inches in diameter. It has structure made of beech, with beech veneer tabletops. The coffee table is made of the same material and shares a similar design. The main differences between them are that the corner table has four legs instead of three, stands lower, and is larger in diameter.

1 The P-021 model coffee table.
2 The Hop-Hop coffee table.
3 When the tabletop is lifted, the Hop-Hop coffee table reveals a well equipped interior.
4 The S-163 model coffee table and corner table.

4

COMMANDING PRESENCE

Some pieces of furniture are impossible to ignore. Their well defined personality and robust, eye-catching shapes make them the center of attention in any room. The nine chairs featured in this section are all noteworthy for their elegant and unique appearance, as well as their practical and comfortable design.

The Only You model, designed by José Camacho, features soft, wavy contours. Its silhouette is reminiscent of a classic park bench.

Dorsus, by Margarita Viarnés, is characterized by its strong, unfrivolous appearance. Straight lines predominate in the design, although the slightly curved back provides a welcome contrast. The chair is made of beech, which may be stained in a variety of colors. The seat may be upholstered in microfiber material or cotton. The Dorsus Contract chair shown in photograph 3 has a similar design with a more youthful, informal look.

In decorative terms an arabesque is an ornate design of intertwined spirals. The Arabesco chair by Pedro Miralles uses this concept to achieve the union of two essential concepts in decoration: comfort and decorative beauty. Its beech structure can be left exposed or upholstered in microfiber material, velvet, or leather.

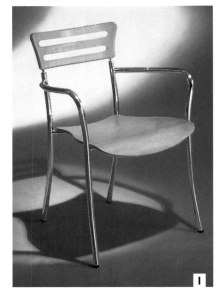

1 The Only You.
2 The Dorsus chair.
3 The Dorsus Contract chair.
4 The Arabesco.
5 The Potro chair.
6 The Margot.
7 The Bárbara.
8 The Bárbara.
9 The Siesta.

The Potro chair by Oscar Tusquets features an unusual pyramid-shaped design. It is available in three sizes and with several kinds of upholstery, such as cotton, microfiber, suede leather, or aniline fiber.

Margot, by Margarita Viarnés, is a singular design composed of curved lines that intertwine through the back, seat, and cloth armrests. The harmonious complexity of its legs gives the chair a different appearance, depending on the angle of sight.

The Bárbara chair and armchair are notable for their single block appearance. The design also features a well balanced combination of curves and slight angles.

The last piece shown is the attractive Siesta model from the Porada collection. This charming rocking chair is a modern version of the old classic.

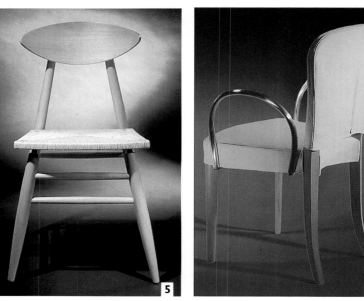

THE BEST CLOSET

A spacious, practical closet is a welcome addition to any home. To fulfill the diverse needs of any family, such a closet should be divided into various compartments, each with its own size and characteristics, and equipped with several bars and drawers. The Studimo and S96 collections provide a wide range of modules and components that can be adapted to meet needs and space constraints. Moreover, both designs feature an strikingly clean look.

Studimo, designed by Team Form Ag, is a flexible collection whose timeless design ensures a lifetime of use. Its various modules are available in a range of heights, widths, and depths so that closets can be configured to suit each person's needs. The collection comes in a variety of lacquered finishes, such as light gray, white, and champagne, as well as natural maple. It also offers a choice of hinged or sliding doors.

Among the most striking elements of the Studimo collection are the large sliding doors made of acid-treated glass. The composition shown in the first photograph combines open and closed modules along with sets of drawers. The finishing touch is provided by the thick panels of acid-treated glass. The third photograph shows a classic bookcase for the living room. The composition contains abundant drawers and hinged cabinets, including a module for the television.

The second photograph shows a closet from the S96 collection, also from Team Form Ag. The S96 closets are notable for their simple, streamlined contours on the outside and their great capacity on the inside. Their design is appropriate for both houses and offices. The model features hinged doors with black or aluminum handles. The available interior components include shelves in various sizes, clothes racks, and sets of drawers in opaque plastic. The insides of the closets are laminated, and the exterior is available in an assortment of lacquered finishes.

The fourth photograph shows part of the interior of an S96 closet with the space divided into two sections. One unique feature is the fold-out tie and belt hangers attached to one of the hinged doors.

1 The Studimo closet. The sliding glass doors can close off the set of drawers.
2 The S96 closet with hinged doors.
3 This Studimo closet includes a module for the television.
4 The S96 closets are completely equipped.
5 Detail view of the opaque plastic drawers of the S96 closets.

STREAMLINED LIGHTING

Modern lighting fixtures are characterized by basic shapes and absolute simplicity of design. The number of pieces is reduced to a bare minimum in an effort to decrease their visual bulk. At the same time, technological innovations have allowed these designs to become more practical and flexible, with adjustable positions and intensity of light. These pieces avoid excessive or ostentatious designs and have the capacity to decorate any corner with absolute discretion.

The first photograph shows the Fucsia lamp designed by A. Castiglioni. This is a triple-piece model composed of fixtures that hang from the ceiling in perfect balance. The base attaches to the ceiling and holds three long cables with cone-shaped lamps at the ends. A long cylinder inside each metal cone holds the halogen bulbs.

The next model featured is the Bloc lamp designed by Rodolfo Dordoni. This elegant ceiling lamp provides a warm, pure light that will brighten any room. It features a metal structure with a shade composed of polycarbonate tessarae. Despite its simplicity, the Bloc model possesses some of the classic beauty of older designs. Its serene and moderate shapes make it appropriate for a wide range of styles, since they blend in discreetly with even the most complicated decorative schemes. The model comes in amber, blue, and green shades and is also available in a tabletop version.

Finally, the third model dealt with in this section is another version of the Fucsia lamp by A. Castiglioni. In this case, the lamp is composed of up to twelve independent spotlights which provide the abundant light necessary for illuminating large rooms. The photograph shows the various individual lamps that make up this fixture. Each of these is fitted with metal rings without bases that establish and bring definition to the diameter.

These lamps are all designed to fulfill specific needs, and they do their jobs flawlessly. No less important is their decorative quality, taken in a slightly different context, each model can be considered an authentic work of art.

1 The Fucsia with three spotlights.
2 The Bloc.
3 The Fucsia with twelve spotlights.

A TOUCH OF ELEGANCE

The furniture shown here, all from the Stua collection, belong to the exclusive group of objects that are striking by their very presence in a room. Original and also practical, these designs shun conventionality and hackneyed clichés, and take a bold leap into the future with daring and innovative shapes and contours.

The Sapporo bookcase, by the Spanish designer Jesús Gasca, is clearly what catches the eye in the first photograph. The Sapporo line is a collection of modules with measurements ranging from one to six times the standard height. Each module rests on a steel base, which can either be fixed or mounted on wheels. The sliding door panels are available either in clear or in acid-treated glass. The result is an exceptionally discreet and practical piece of furniture adaptable to the size of nearly any room as if made to order, and yet providing plenty of storage space. The model shown has white-lacquered edges and sliding glass doors tinted in a light shade of green. Sturdy steel legs provide support for this elegantly designed bookcase.

The second photograph shows the original Malena armchair, designed by Jon Gasca. This model is remarkable for its simple yet inviting contours, as well as for the delicate latticework on its back. The chair's structure is solid beech, and the upholstery on the seat and back cushions can easily be removed for cleaning. Interestingly, this armchair features aluminum legs and front wheels.

Egoa, by Josep Mora, is a classic of modern design. It offers unparalleled comfort thanks to its specially designed adjustable backrest that yields to accommodate body movements. The chair features a metal structure that comes in chrome or black finish, and the seat is available either upholstered or in wood.

The third photograph is of an attractive and fully equipped dining room. In the background is the Sapporo bookcase described above, and in the foreground, the Zero table by Jesús Gasca. This table, available in round and square versions, features a single, aluminum foot connected to a steel base. The tabletop can be ordered in a variety of materials, although the most popular version is made of cherry wood.

The chairs are Globus, also by Jesús Gasca. These light, stackable chairs feature comfortable, inviting contours with a curved seat and a backrest that follows the shape of the back to give a feeling of deep relaxation. The original lines of this model make it perfect for a fresh and informal style of interior design. The tubular steel structure supports a seat and backrest available in cherry, beech, ash, or maple.

1 The star of this photograph is the Sapporo bookcase.
2 The Malena armchair.
3 The Egoa chair
4 Dining room featuring the Sapporo book case, Zero table, and Globus chairs.

ESSENTIAL STORAGE SPACE

Everyone accumulates countless objects over a lifetime: books, souvenirs, or decorative objects from family inheritances. The problem is always to find space for storing these objects in a neat, organized way. Some unique or attractive pieces deserve to be on display, while others may be hidden away. What is needed is a well designed piece of furniture for storing all of these treasured possessions.

Studimo, by Team Form Ag, was designed specifically to meet these storage needs. This collection of modular bookcases and cabinets combines a classic style with unrivaled flexibility and variety. The collection was revised in 1996 to respond to recent trends and also so that its selection of components would be more complete.

The Studimo line offers limitless configurations because its well balanced collection of components can be combined to produce anything from small dressing tables or wardrobes to wall-to-wall bookcases.

Included in this practical collection are features such as sliding doors, glass panels, drawers, and shelves. The components are available in several lacquered finishes, including light gray, white, and champagne, as well as natural maple.

The first photograph shows a classic, wall-to-wall bookcase divided into numerous compartments. At the center of the composition is a set of drawers. The two sliding plates of acid-treated glass shown in the photograph serve partly to protect the structure.

The second bookcase leaves only two sections open, one horizontal and one vertical. The rest of the shelves are hidden behind hinged, lacquered doors. The lower part of the bookcase contains a small set of drawers.

The third photograph shows a spacious display case that has been divided horizontally. This model features metal edges and front panels made of acid-treated glass.

1

2

1 Wall-to-wall bookcase divided into numerous compartments. The panels of acid-treated glass create an eye-catching effect.

2 Most of the columns in this bookcase are hidden behind hinged, lacquered doors.

3 A spacious display case that has been divided horizontally.

THE EMPIRE OF DESIGN

So-called Design pieces are pieces of furniture whose designs seem especially intended to break away from tradition. These pieces have their own way of interpreting reality; they transform it and mold it according to their own criteria. Their shapes are impressive, their textures surprising, and their colors stimulate the senses. The furniture featured here helps in understanding this concept of design.

Lamps are pieces that are often given an innovative, avant-garde treatment. The first photograph shows the Soda model by Jonathan Daifuku. This lamp is available in floor, ceiling, and wall versions. The diffuser is made of hand-blown opal glass which has been treated with acid. The floor model features a rotating lampshade. The support for the lampshade has a chrome finish, and the base and tube come in metallic gray.

The second photograph features an exceptionally original design, the Sensual Pampa armchair designed by Cappellini. This piece possesses a light, minimal metal structure and a richly padded body. The seat is a flat, narrow piece, while the back is a wavy rectangular piece which adapts itself to the curves of the back. Two open holes in the back serve to break up the design and prevent monotony.

On warm summer nights, nothing could be better than to spend a few relaxing hours in the Knock-out chaise longue designed by T. Colzani. The structure of this model is made of metal, which is available painted in textured black, silver, or sand tones. This base supports numerous solid chestnut rods. This model is available with cushions and armrests made of Sanforized cotton.

The Volo model, designed by T. Zappa and M. Marconato, is a light, airy bookcase made of cherry. The shelves are made of metal with a tarnished silver or antique green finish and are also available in acid-treated glass with polished edges. The legs are made of copper-colored brass. This piece can be ordered leaning to the right or to the left.

1

2

1 The Soda lamp.
2 The Sensual Pampa armchair.
3 The Knock-out chaise longue.
4 The Soda lamp.

4

The bookcases shown here all offer new solutions for storage. These innovative models remedy the lack of space that plagues many homes, and at the same time, they present a look that makes a clean break with the sometimes stodgy image of the bookcase. Because of this, they are especially well suited to a young, informal style of design, where more traditional models would seem out of place.

The first three pieces belong to the 606 line designed by Dieter Rams. This collection is an all-purpose system of shelves made of anodized aluminum, which can be adapted to a wide range of sizes and styles.

The first photograph shows a massive composition extending from wall to wall, made up of a many shelves separated by vertical columns. This immense, hanging structure stops just short of the floor,

firmly and captivatingly suspended in space. The abundant storage capacity of this arrangement makes it suitable for offices as well as homes.

The second photograph features an arrangement created specifically for offices. Although its silver tone is identical to the previous model, it includes several new components. The large drawers and containers in various sizes and shapes make this design the ideal solution for various storage needs.

As mentioned above, this line is equally suitable for homes and offices. The third photograph shows a large area, which could also be a library or conference room. In this case, the bookcase does not rest against the wall, but rather constitutes a wall in itself. Support is provided by sturdy steel columns anchored to the floor. Since the shelves have no back, the rest of

the room can be seen through the bookcase. This design is ideal for partially separating a room into two areas without sacrificing the feeling of spaciousness and light.

Finally, a highly practical model is shown in the fourth photograph. This compact and attractive design is the Server model by Cozza and Mascheroni. This original piece provides an efficient space for a computer and the many items that go with it. Server features a steel structure and various metal plaques, as well as a wooden table for holding the keyboard. It comes with wheels for easy movement

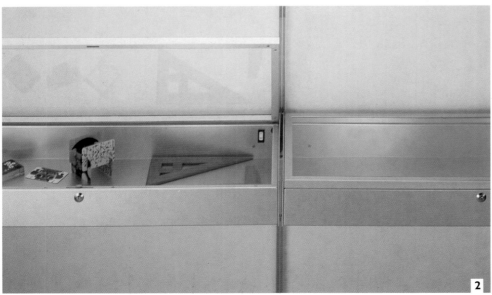

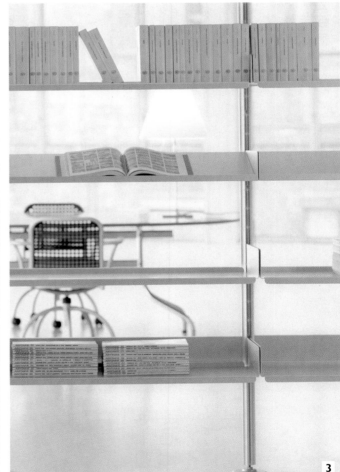

1   A wall-to-wall arrangement from the 606 collection.

2   The satin-finished interior of the drawers from the 606 collection.

3   This bookcase rests on sturdy steels legs.

4   The Server model, for computers.

COMFORT AND BALANCE

The chairs featured in this chapter all share original and innovative designs. Nevertheless, they also manage to maintain a touch of classicism and avoid a stridently avant-garde appearance. As a result, these pieces are modern but at the same time discrete enough to fit in with a wide range of decorative styles without causing esthetic conflicts or contrasts.

The first photograph shows the Marilin chair designed by Ximo Roca. This elegant and well-balanced chair is characterized by its exceptionally light appearance and the remarkable comfort it affords. It features a frame made of steel tubing with a metallic finish and a plywood seat. The back is available in woven pith or polypropylene. The polypropylene version can be decorated with a serigraph.

Maia is another design by Ximo Roca. This chair is made of beech wood and features a comfortable back with woven cotton bands. The back is available with a removable slipcover that gives additional personality to the design. The beechwood seat can also be upholstered.

For a young informal style of decor, the colorful Nil chair, also by Ximo Roca, is the ideal choice. The rounded shapes of this stackable chair give this design an innocent, almost naive character. The frame is made of chromed steel tubing, and the seat consists of a piece of curved plywood. The back is available in wood or pith. The different types of veneer used in the plywood can be combined with various colors of pith to produce a wide range of combinations.

Finally, the Dolly chair is a foldable model designed by Antonio Citterio and Oliver Loew. This exceptional design has a fiberglass frame that has been reinforced with polypropylene. The seat can be made of the same material or bleached beech wood. The seat can be upholstered, and the chair is available in a variety of colors.

1 The Marilin chair.
2 The Maia chair.
3 The Nil chair.
4 The Dolly chair.

3

4

PLANT FIBER

Plant fiber is a warm and flexible material. It can be used to make any kind of furniture, since its flexibility lends itself to the creation of new and unusual shapes. This material is quickly finding its place in modern furniture design.

This versatile fiber can be used in manufacturing tables, footstools, stools, and rugs, as well as in wall and ceiling coverings. One of its most valuable qualities is its outstanding airiness, which makes it ideal for bringing an open, uncluttered look to a room. Its light color and warm feel make it the perfect way to add a young, informal touch to a decor.

The first photograph shows a streamlined chair with an elegantly simple design based on curved contours. An arched metal bar constitutes both the leg and armrest. The seat and back are formed by a single curved piece.

The design of the chair in the second photograph is exemplary for its balance. The chair's frame consists of a metal tube divided into two parallel halves. The same tube continues until it reaches the floor and becomes the curved legs of the chair. The chair achieves perfect balance through a carefully engineered distribution of weight. Plant fiber makes the ideal covering for an irregular surface like this one; it adjusts perfectly to the snaking contours of the chair.

The third photograph features a footrest with a certain classical touch. While it is reminiscent of the old upholstered models with intricately carved legs, the use of plant fiber gives it an up-to-date look. The result is a lighter, more agile version of an old classic.

The chair pictured in the fourth photograph makes a clean break with anything seen so far. It combines wood and plant fiber and presents a well balanced combination of straight and curved lines.

As can easily be seen in the fifth and sixth photographs, plant fiber can also be used with armchairs and sofas. Thanks to this new material, these two traditional pieces take on a completely new and current look.

1 The key features of this chair are the curved bars at the front, which act as both legs and armrests.

2 A carefully engineered distribution of weight ensures balance in this chair.

3 Plant fiber brings this classic piece up to date.

4 This chair features an attractive combination of straight and curved lines.

5 An armchair with a traditional look.

6 Sofas made with plant fiber are perfect for a young, informal style of decoration.

INSEPARABLE COMPANIONS

Some pieces of furniture possess a certain bravura that makes them the center of attention in any room they occupy. They stand out among the rest of the decor and have enough character and aplomb to define the overall personality of the room. However, just as important as the more dominant pieces are the supporting actors in the design of an interior. These pieces are the inseparable companions for the centerpieces mentioned earlier.

Our first selection is an elegant and practical closet designed by Alberto Lievore & Associates. This svelte, sober cabinet provides an efficient system for organizing folded shirts. It rests on wheels and features a unique system of dual hinged doors, each of which opens up a different side of the cabinet. The interior holds two large, extractable trays, as well as a drawer for complements. A mirror is also included, along with tie hangers on each door. The cabinet measures 50 x 172 x 50 centimeters (approximately 20 x 20 x 68 inches) and is available in the following finishes: hazel, salmon, walnut, and mahogany.

The second photograph features a modern version of the classic dining room buffet designed by Lievore & Associates. This model is part of a complete collection of living room and dining room furniture. The body of this refined piece of furniture rests on sturdy cylindrical legs. The side doors open at an angle, leaving space for storing bottles. The cover hides a drawer which can be upholstered for keeping silverware. The legs are adjustable, and the metal fittings are made of steel and solid brass. It measures 210 by 80 by 46 centimeters (approximately 83 by 31 by 18 inches) and is available in natural, salmon, walnut, and mahogany finishes.

An innovative telephone set is shown in the third photograph. This model was designed by Pedro Miralles. Its size makes it ideal for entrances, hallways, and living rooms. The set is composed of two cabinets with a door and drawer, and a curved, cushioned bench. The rounded legs are made of wood. The piece comes with hazel, salmon, walnut, or mahogany finishes. It measures 35 by 76 by 35 centimeters (approximately 14 by 30 by 14 inches).

1 Shirt closet.
2 A classic dining room buffet.
3 Telephone set.

1

2

3

ARTISTIC LIGHTING

Lamps and other fixtures illuminate our lives. The lamps included in this section are evident artistic representations, and as such, they are esthetically pleasing. Their creators have executed them daringly, searching for new shapes.

The first design is inspired on the subtle undulations of ocean waves. The Crescendo model, designed by J. Daifuku, is made up of individual lamps that can be connected togeth-

er. Each module is made of extruded aluminum and is painted gray.

The second model is the surprising Veroca soffit, which comprises an array of fluorescent ceiling lights, hidden behind a textile shade, which comes in white, yellow, green, or blue.

The classic table lamp acquires a new character with Conica, designed by Joan Casanyes. This model comprises a conically-shaped polyester and paper shade supported by an aluminum base, also conical. The base comes in gray, red, green, blue, golden, or copper. The screen is sold in white or amber.

Photograph 4, designed by Toni Arola, shows a stylized and original ceiling lamp. The Nimba base is a glass hoop encircled by a second metallic hoop that hangs from the ceiling, supported by a pair of strong, tensed cables.

Along more classical lines is the Copa, by Barnal and Isern. Copa is hung from the ceiling, and its base is divided into three branches. A translucent white opaline glass shade is mounted on each one of the

branches. The structure is metallic and comes in a bronze or nickel finish.

The Bloc design, by Rodolfo Dordoni, is a table lamp that produces diffuse lighting. Its shade is made of multiple polycarbonate tesserae of various colors (amber, white, blue, and green).

Finally, the Plomada model, designed by Pete Sans, is a ceiling lamp, and has a pulley system which allows the lamp to be hoisted or lowered to the desirable height.

1 Crescendo appliance.
2 Veroca soffit.
3 Conica table lamps.
4 Nimba ceiling lamp.
5 Copa ceiling lamp.
6 Bloc table lamp.
7 Plomada lamp.

106

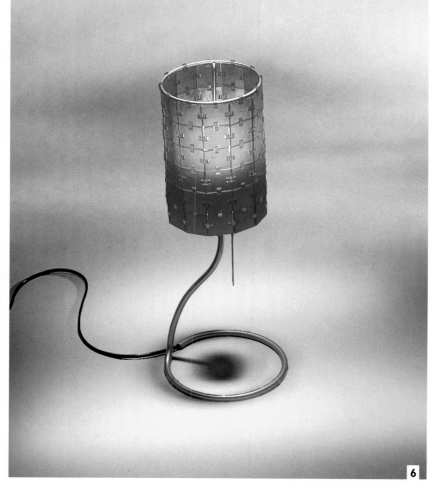

S T U D Y   T I M E

Furniture for work or study should primarily be for providing a practical work area that makes the best possible use of available space and facilitates several types of activities. Contemporary design includes models for every taste, from classic desks to minimalist designs. Some designs offer a number of small containers to organize a diverse collection of office materials, while others are reminiscent of the familiar school desk from years ago.

The first photograph features the Secreter model designed by M. A. Ciganda. This desk belongs to the Piezas collection, a complete line of exclusive furniture that brings a fresh look to the classics.

The Nobel desk by Jaime Tresserra is shown flanked by a pair of pivoting cabinets. This practical set is made of walnut with stainless steel fittings. The cabinet on the left includes a slide-out pencil box, as well as three drawers. The cabinet on the right contains a sliding extension and a filing cabinet. The writing surface, pencil case, and drawers are covered with calf's leather, as are the top and front pieces of the cabinets.

The Carpett model also by Jaime Tresserra, is a secretary in walnut that has been varnished in a light tone. The interior is made of natural sycamore, with fittings consisting of pig-leather straps and metal rods coated with silver wash.

The exceptionally cleanly contoured and graceful model is also a great space-saver; it folds up neatly when not in use.

Another design by Jaime Tresserra is the original Carlton-house Butterfly model made of walnut with a natural sycamore interior. The metal fittings have a sulfurated nickel finish. When closed, this practical model is almost flat, and when opened it creates a unique butterfly effect.

The Paralelas executive desk, also by Jaime Tresserra, is made of walnut and features a sliding extension, cut glass container and portfolio. Straps of hand-sewn peccary leather bring a touch of distinction to this attractive design.

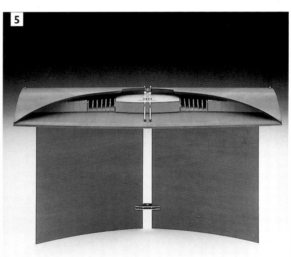

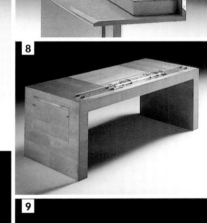

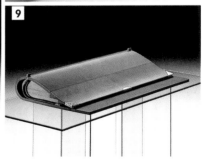

1 The Secreter model.
2 The Nobel desk.
3 A practical cabinet on wheels.
4 The Carpett model, open.
5 The Carlton-house Butterfly model, open.

6 Auxiliary cabinets from the Tensor and Paralelas line.
7 The Carlton-house Butterfly model, closed.
8 The Paralelas executive desk.
9 The Carpett model, closed.

PRACTICAL AND FUNTIONAL

The chairs pictured here solve a variety of interior design problems. Some of the chairs are light and compact, and are therefore ideal for confined areas. Others, with invitingly enveloping shapes, emphasize comfort.

Abanica, designed by Oscar Tusquets, is a stackable chair featuring elegant, cleanly defined contours. Subtle innovations give the chair an unusual and original appearance without being strident or shocking. The metal

frame is carefully and efficiently designed. It supports the backrest and gives visual definition to the seat, and then extends to meet two legs shaped like bow ties. The body of the chair consists of two wicker pieces shaped like truncated triangles, which make up the seat and backrest. Both pieces are slightly curved at the ends, giving the chair a relaxed, comfortable look.

1

2

3

1 The Abanica chair.
2 This chair's most outstanding quality is its simplicity.
3 The Achemilla chair.
4 Three exceptional designs characterized by their classic appearance.

The second photograph shows the 40502 model chair. This model is notable for its simplicity. The metal frame is only visible in the legs, which are bent into a bow shape and connected to each other by a bar at the middle. The body of this stackable chair is composed of one piece of wickerwork that acts as both a seat and backrest.

Another stackable model is shown in the third photograph. The Achemilla chair, designed by Miki Astori, is a comfortable chair characterized by its soft, curved lines. The metal frame features straight legs in the front and slightly curved ones in the back for increased stability. The one-piece body is made of soft and durable plant fiber.

The fourth photograph shows three exceptional pieces: two comfortable padded armchairs with a service table between them. The white sofa is the Bob model and features straight lines, a low back and large, sturdy armrests. A cylindrical cushion provides back support. The black sofa (Poggiapiedi Carlo) is similar in appearance, but the back reclines and the seat can be moved forward. The table is supported by crossed metal legs and has a top made of plant fiber.

SUBTLE SHAPES

The first model shown is the Paspartous table. This attractive design is based on the superimposition of two planes. It is made of cherry, and the top surface is available in white lacquer or in cherry, as well. The table includes a lower shelf and a glass cover.

The Lira I chair owes its remarkable elegance to its gently curved back, composed of several wave-shaped slats. It is made of cherry and comes with various types of upholstery.

1 The Paspartous table.
2 The Lira I chair
3 The Taula table.
4 The Nido model.
5 The Macarena armchair.
6 The Andrea armchair and sofa.

The pieces of furniture featured on the following pages all belong to the Taller collection designed by José Martinez Medina. These subtle, simple, and sophisticated designs are the antithesis of mass-produced furniture. Both their appearance and their careful construction make them unique pieces that give an air of distinction to any room. The various models that make up the collection can be shuffled to suit individual tastes.

The Macarena armchair is an especially fresh and original design. Its informal shape and brightly colored upholstery cannot fail to grab attention. This upholstered armchair features naturally colored beech arms and rear wheels of the same material.

Finally, the Andrea armchair and sofa offer a surprisingly balanced design with a warm, inviting feel. These densely cushioned models have wooden front legs and sturdy, metal rear supports.

5

An ideal table for large gatherings is the Taula model. A strong, metal frame with rails, located underneath, allows the table to be easily adjusted to different lengths. The process for extending the table could not be simpler; when the legs are pulled apart the extension boards are revealed. A mere turn of these boards puts them in the proper place. The result is a perfectly designed table without an obtrusive central column. The legs are made of cherry, and two of them have wheels to make extending the table easier.

The Nido model, in turn, consists of three beech tables that fit perfectly atop one another. These decorative pieces are stained in a cherry wood color.

6

7

COVERING WALLS

Shelves cover and adorn walls, concealing their architectural imperfections, and can be considered the best type of storage space. Modern interior design evades classical single-unit bookcases, since they occupy a considerable amount of space. The new system of modules and hanging shelves, on the other hand, "decongests" rooms, thus bringing them a younger and lighter appearance.

The star of this section is the Prologo bookcase, designed by Jaime Tresserra. It is a modular bookcase made of walnut. Its fittings and accessories are made of stainless steel. This model, shown in photograph 1, is a wall-to-wall structure. The shelves are connected together by vertical wood panels forming a perfect symmetrical framework. From the two central shelves, unusual leaves or flaps can be pulled out and used to consult books. A sliding staircase is attached to a rail which extends from one end of the top shelf to the other. Metal plates can be fixed to the corners, with

engraved reference numbers or letters, in order to allow the user to locate books with ease. The Prólogo bookcases are wired up inside so that lamps can be installed within them. Attached to the staircase are leather pouches, provided as temporary storage space for books that are retrieved from, or replaced on, the top shelves.

Another light bookcase, noted for its elegance and highly modern design, is the Ulm by Enzo Mari. The most prominent features are its simple forms and perfect anchorage.

Finally, the Pab bookcase, designed by Kairos Studios, is made up of a long piece of wood, which is partially collapsible, supported by extremely light cords. When necessary, the structure can be folded up. This system also includes glass panels that enclose the storage spaces and special cubby holes for small objects.

114

1 Prologo bookcase, built from wall to wall.
2 Ulm bookcase.
3 The Ulm´s anchorage system.
4 Librería "Pab".
5 The Prologo´s leather pouch.
6 One of the Prologo´s pull-out leaves.

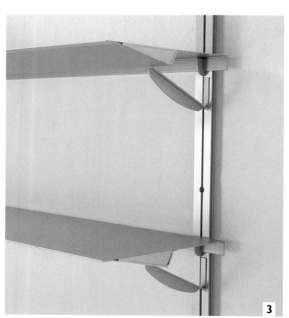

2

SWEET DREAMS

To ensure a good night's sleep, a spring mattress should rest on a firm, well designed base. The beds featured here are all characterized by their durable structures and their balanced and harmonious shapes. However, they are more than mere supports for mattresses. They also enhance the bedroom decor.

Though some still prefer more ostentatious models, with carved wood or wrought iron structures topped with imposing canopies, contemporary interior design tends toward discretion. Designers favor bedrooms with simple, tidy shapes and predominantly straight lines. Canopies are generally avoided and headboards tend to be inconspicuous. This furniture is generally made of natural, high-quality materials.

The most notable characteristic of the first Greta is its headboard. This original and attractive piece is composed of two slightly curved panels attached to one another. Three long grooves run along the panels, adding a personal touch. A classic night table with polished surfaces flanks the bed.

The Argo is a contemporary piece that can fit with a broad range of decorative styles. It has no end-piece, and its headboard has delicate-looking lines. This headboard consists of a light frame containing two squares of unvarnished wood decorated with small grooves to form a geometric pattern. The design of this interior is completed by a chest of three drawers with a slightly rounded front, along with two similar night tables.

The Zanzibar rests on simple, cone-shaped legs. The one-piece headboard is made up of several vertical slats framed by a broad wooden molding.

1 The Greta.
2 The Argo.
3 The Zanzibar.

1

2

3

PURE SIMPLICITY

1 The Shine dining room table with two Flower armchairs.
2 The Shine desk with the Silver chair.
3 The Scrittarello desk.

Because work tables and dining room tables serve different functions, they are usually found in different areas of the home, and each may have to blend in with different types decorative styles. Dining room tables are often a focal point for the social life of a family. A work table, on the other hand, is generally used by only one person at a time.

Presented here are examples of dining room tables and work tables, all of which are notable for their utmost simplicity and for the strength and clarity of their forms.

The Shine model, designed by Vico Magistretti, captures some of the polish and glamour of a former era. Its contours are simple yet impeccably balanced and its volumes conform masterfully to traditional esthetic principles. Its stainless steel legs add

a touch of originality to the design. The legs rise from the floor at a slight angle until they join a crossbar near the base. This structure is crowned by a round tabletop which is available in maple or in white laminate. The table is accompanied by two youthful Flower armchairs with bright orange upholstery applied over a steel structure.

New technologies, such as computers, the Internet, and fax machines allow workers to communicate with their office, or even with other parts of the world, without leaving home. As a result, many of today's homes have a room specifically dedicated to work. However, these rooms are not decorated in the dull, gray tones typical of offices, but rather with a touch of youthful exuberance. The second photograph shows the Shine desk accompanied by the Silver chair. The

Shine desk shares many of the characteristics of the dining room table described above. The legs are similar, although they are further separated than in the dining room table, and the tabletop is rectangular rather than round. The Silver chair has a steel frame and body. Its most outstanding features are its legs, which arch downward from the seat and are fitted with wheels. Both the seat and back are made of steel latticework.

Another practical model is the Scrittarello desk designed by Achille Castiglioni. This remarkably efficient desk is completely collapsible, thanks to the scissor-like action of its legs. These legs can also support additional platforms to provide more storage space. The rectangular tabletop is made of laminated wood for easy cleaning.

The West, too restless to be satisfied with its own designs, often looks to the exotic in search of inspiration. In a world where everything seems already to have been invented, originality is an often hard-to-attain ideal, and improvisation is unfeasible. Therefore, the West turns eastward to absorb the art and even the mundane objects that have been created by East Asia's seemingly eternal culture. The design of the furniture featured here strives for the beauty and functionability so characteristic of Japanese furniture, while at the same time adapting the furniture to today's trends and needs.

Japanese furniture is notable for its exquisite beauty, attention to detail, and exceptionally delicate forms. Samuro, designed by Jaime Tresserra, is a sophisticated cabinet that captures some of the essence of Japanese art. In the Far East, a piece of furniture is traditionally considered a sign of identity, an inseparably personal object linked to a place in the social hierarchy. Tresserra has managed to capture this spirit and bring it closer to the Western way of thinking, yet without changing the intrinsic Eastern quality of the pieces. Samuro is a double-bodied cabinet made of walnut treated with clear varnish. Featuring sulfurized metal fittings, the piece has an exceptionally discreet and modest appearance when closed. When open, it reveals a large number of small compartments. Its delicate exterior covers a deeply practical interior.

The Madia model is a handsome wardrobe with hinged doors. It is available in a wide range of finishes and measures 87 by 45 by 154 centimeters (34 by 18 by 61 inches). This classically shaped piece stands on prism-shaped legs. The key element of its appearance is the molding on the top, whose angled corners are reminiscent of the roof of a pagoda.

134

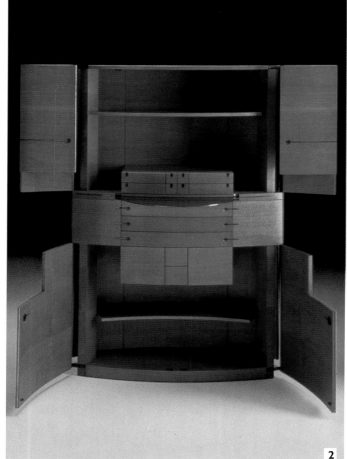

1 *The Samuro cabinet.*

2 *The interior of the Samuro cabinet is full of small, independent compartments.*

3 *The Madia.*

A TOUCH OF THE UNUSUAL

In interior design, only a few details are often enough to achieve a brilliant effect. A few exceptional pieces, carefully chosen and judiciously placed, can be highly effective. The furniture shown here falls into this category. Their designs are the result of a new spirit in design, where beauty and function blend in perfect harmony.

The Desta armchair was designed by M. Marconato and T. Zappa. This model is characterized by its sinuous contours, which create an effect that is almost sensual. The front legs slant forward, while the rear legs, stretching out to form the armrests, slant gracefully backward. The frame is made of solid cherry, available in various finishes. The seat and back can come upholstered in plant fiber, as well as in an abundant selection of fabrics. The upholstery shown in the photograph is a contemporary pattern which imitates spotted cowhide.

The next photograph features the Isetta chair and the Isotta armchair. These comfortably cushioned models are available in several versions, such as single- or double-thick seat, or with legs that are hidden under the upholstery or completely visible. The legs can be finished in various tones.

The Monza armchair, designed by Giuseppe Terragni, features a truly revolutionary design. Created for the fourth Monza Bienniale competition, this unique armchair features a beech frame along with a curved sheet of veneer varnished in a Corynth tone. The cushions are filled with polyurethane foam with velvet upholstery.

The Olga easy chair is made of beech and can be upholstered in various materials. This model is ideal for waiting rooms or conference rooms. It features a handle on the back for portability. To save space, these chairs can also be stacked as high as four units.

1 The Desta model.
2 The Isetta chair and the Isotta armchair.
3 The Monza chair.
4 The Olga model.

4

MAGICAL MODELS

The models featured here are all the product of only a few parts, some high-quality materials, and a unique design. These are remarkable pieces of furniture despite of their apparent simplicity, or perhaps because of it. They are conservative with space and fulfill practical needs, but they also lend an innovative and attractive look to a room. For these reasons, they are fine examples of contemporary design.

The first model, Tome 3, is a simply designed bookcase composed of only five pieces. Its key components are two lacquered steel frames and three shelves made of walnut veneer. The steel structure provides reliable support for the shelves, which have metal guides for the books.

Easy is an armchair characterized by an unusually compact yet inviting shape. Its soft contours make it ideal for a youthful, informal style of interi-

or design. This chair stands on lacquered steel legs and features a wooden frame that can be upholstered in various materials. The upholstery is completely removable for easy cleaning. The Easy sofa shares the same design as the armchair and is available in various sizes.

Asseyez-vous and Assieds-toi are two light and unelaborate models that function both as tables and benches. Their firm, straight appearance is a result of their sturdy lacquered steel structure. When used with accompanying cushions, Asseyez-vous and Assieds-toi become a double or single bench, respectively. The upholstery on the cushions is completely removable. Removing the cushions turns these practical models into coffee tables.

The Metalle chair is characterized by its solid, exquisitely balanced shapes. The originality of this design lies in its long legs, extended seat and short

backrest. This model is manufactured in lacquered steel.

Finally, the Malabar is a backless bench that achieves a maximum of beauty from a minimum of components. It consists of a simple structure of lacquered steel tubing holding a rectangular cushion. The upholstery can be removed to facilitate cleaning.

1 The Tome 3 bookcase.
2 The Easy armchair.
3 The Easy sofa.
4 The Asseyez-vous bench and coffee table.
5 The Assieds-toi bench and coffee table.
6 The Metalle chair.
7 The Malabar backless bench.

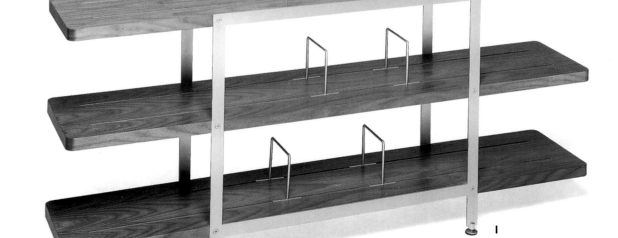

FOUR SPLENDID SOFAS

When it comes to sofas, everyone has a particular preference. Some people prefer the traditional sofa with its cozy, enveloping shapes. Others favor more contemporary designs. In fact, as long as the sofa is scaled in proportion to the room that surrounds it, all options are equally valid. Nothing detracts more from the impact of an interior's design than a sofa that is disproportionately large or small. Creating an ambiance that goes with the style of these pieces, often the focal points of the living room, is of primary importance.

The Raffles line, designed by Vico Magistretti, chooses a tasteful point midway between classical and modern. Its contours are straight, clean, and well proportioned, and it features soft armrests and an especially thick cushion on the seat. It rests on wooden legs with wheels. The complete collection includes an armchair, a pouf, and a two or three-seat sofa, all of which come with goose-down cushions. The models shown in the photograph are upholstered with durable, stain-resistant material in an off-white color.

The second photograph shows the Chesterfield couch, a traditional example of exquisite taste. Its deep seat and raised back guarantee excellent support and help the person sitting in the sofa to avoid bad posture. The backrest is joined with the armrests and is padded with a singularly shaped cushion that gives this traditional sofa its unique personality. The inner sections of the back and armrests feature an exceptionally elaborate pattern of upholstery.

The Welcome model, designed by Michele Sbrogiò, is a sofa with removable upholstery. This piece has a strong personality. It combines exceptional comfort with a remarkably light appearance, and features an aluminum structure lacquered in a flat steel tone. Its inviting, heavily cushioned body rises gracefully on streamlined aluminum legs, leaving its tantalizingly comfortable cushions in the foreground.

Finally, the Tiglio by Marino Ramazzotti is a compact sofa with a straight back connected to the armrests. It features a rigid base with cushions arranged harmoniously on top.

1 The Raffles sofa.
2 The Chesterfield model.
3 The Welcome sofa.
4 The Tiglio sofa.

3

4

DELICATE ELEGANCE

Delicate and apparently fragile, these tables give off an air of exceptional refinement and beauty. The sheer simplicity of their design captivates the observer with gentle, perfectly balanced contours that shun brusque, aggressive innovation. This noble simplicity makes them equally at home in formal salons and youthful, casual surroundings.

Oval tables provide ample useable space while taking up less room than their round or square counterparts. An example of this is the More design by Andreas Weber. This exceptionally innovative table was designed for optimal practicality. Its perfectly balanced shape and soft, molded contours bring a special charm to this light, minimalist design. Its lacquered aluminum structure consists of two firm, straight crossbars connected by delicately curved pieces. Long, svelte, cylindrical legs descend from this structure. One of the most attractive features of this model is its tabletop, composed of a plate of transparent glass flanked by two translucent pieces. The More table can be easily extended and measures 180 or 260 by 110 by 75 centimeters (71 or 102 by 43 by 30 inches).

The Wiz model, designed by Sigla, belongs to a line of tables notable for their fresh design. The casual appearance of this model makes it ideal for the younger members of the family. Its aluminum legs support a frame of varnished beech, reminiscent of a painter's easel. A softly curved tabletop rests on this simple, sturdy structure, with an indentation in the center that could be considered the design's signature. The tabletop is available in translucent glass or laminated in various colors.

1 The More.
2 The Wiz.

2

NATURAL HARMONY

The shapes that prevail in these models follow classical design principles. They are all based on a sharp sense of balance and a harmonious juxtaposition of shapes and volumes. These designs shun garishly novel forms in favor of an austere understatement that relies on pure, uncluttered shapes, natural wood tones, and high-quality materials.

The Pablo Sideboard model is a quietly restrained piece designed by Anna Flötotto, with a central set of drawers flanked by two hinged doors. This design is characterized by its clean, straight lines. It exudes a subtle, rustic flavor.

The second photograph features a wainscot bookcase constructed with the Potter-System collection. This line includes a wide range of modules in various types and tones of wood. This exceptionally flexible collection permits unlimited combinations. The model shown in the second photograph includes a lateral display case notable for its modest metal structure.

Gracia Houssenthl, also designed by Anna Flötotto, is a casual and delicate chair with a wrought iron structure. This chair can come upholstered with plant fiber or it can come covered with a canvas slipcover, as shown in the third photograph.

The fourth model, Ritz, by Birgit Gämmerler, is a modern interpretation of the classic sideboard. The body of this refined piece consists of a central cabinet flanked by two lateral compartments. All three sections feature hinged doors, the side ones made of wood and the central one made of translucent glass. Enough room is left at the top for two spacious drawers. The sideboard rests gracefully on angular metal legs.

Another composition constructed with the Potter-System is shown in the fifth photograph. This piece employs a wide range of modules, including long, narrow modules, floor pieces, drawers, and shelves.

1 The Pablo Sideboard model.
2 A wainscot bookcase constructed with the Potter-System collection.
3 The Gracia Houssenthl chair.

4 The Ritz sideboard.
5 A composition constructed with the Potter-System collection.

SIMPLICITY AND GRACE

Clean, simple, and graceful are some of the adjectives that come to mind when contemplating the chairs featured here. Their strong, tasteful, and perfectly balanced contours favor simplicity over ornamentation, avoiding superfluous adornment.

The first model shown is the Eletta chair by Roberto Barbieri. This warm and youthful design is noteworthy for its extremely slender structure, which is nevertheless extremely sturdy. The design makes consistent use of straight lines, and its frame is made of beech, which can be varnished or stained to a cherry wood tone. The back comes in a wide range of materials, including plant fiber. The chair is available with or without armrests.

The Marsina armchair, designed by Tamar Ben David, is characterized by its snug, rounded contours. Its steel frame comes with an attractive chrome finish, and its upholstery features a handsome and innovative combination of leather and fabric. A charming bow at the back contributes to the unique personality of this chair.

Another surprising design is Temps, a chair so streamlined that it almost disappears when looked at from the side. This chair, designed by Jorge Pensi, is perfect for a fresh, informal style of interior design that puts a premium on space. This stackable model is available with or without armrests, and its frame can be made of beech or cherry. The seat and back are made of molded plywood, and can also be upholstered.

Finally, the Agora model, by Bernal and Isern, is an ideal model for schools, auditoriums, or conference rooms, although also appropriate in private residences. Chrome plated tubes are soldered to a T-shaped base made of one piece of plywood with beech veneer. The seat is composed of a piece of molded beech veneer plywood. It is available with a natural beech finish or stained in various colors, and can also be upholstered in several materials.

146

1 The Eletta model, without armrests.
2 The Marsina model.
3 A charming bow puts the finishing touch on this Marsina chair.
4 The Temps model.
5 The Eletta model, with armrests.
6 The Agora model.

1

2

3

4

DISTINGUISHED SHAPES

1 The Dixie.
2 The Locarno.
3 The Swing.
4 The Square.

Sofas are usually located in the most prestigious parts of a home. They constitute an essential part of the decor and welcome visitors with their invitingly comfortable appearance. In a sense, these pieces of furniture are the calling cards of a house, since their design is a statement about the taste and personality of their owners. Those who like to be part of the avant-garde will choose joltingly innovative models with daring, vivid upholstery. Others prefer a minimalist approach, with more restrained, austere pieces. Finally, there are those who favor a sophisticated, distinguished style, inspired by the classics.

The first piece examined in this section is Dixie, designed by Mauro Lipparini. This is a minimalist, one-piece model, perfect for sparsely furnished rooms with plenty of open space. This piece is available with aluminum legs, giving it a clean, unruffled look; or wooden legs, which add a warm touch of class to the design.

The Locarno model, designed by Marino Ramazzotti, has a refreshingly stylish and tasteful appearance. In spite of its large size, this piece seems light and graceful, thanks to its carefully designed upholstery, soft contours, and off-white color. Its slender, cylindrical legs remain almost completely hidden beneath the body.

The Swing model, designed by Mauro Lipparini, is ideal for youthful nonconformists. This hollow sofa has a distinctly Mediterranean feel. The seat consists of single cushion, whose soft, abundant padding is synonymous with rest and relaxation. The back is made up of several cushions in various sizes.

The last model shown here is Square, by Enrico Franzolini. Like the Locarno model, this design is attractive, harmonious, and well balanced. Its wooden frame is padded with resilient polyurethane foam in various densities, along with polyester fiber. Its legs are made of chromed steel and can also be ordered in varnished wood. The seat and back cushions are filled with polyurethane foam and polyester fiber.

INTERIOR CAPACITY

The need for abundant storage space for books, records, and other objects does not diminish over time. On the contrary, our collection of personal effects tends to grow continually, making convenient, organized storage space an absolute necessity. Modern lifestyles, however, present us with a contradiction. As our storage needs grow, the space available shrinks. Designers have tackled this problem imaginatively, creating furniture with ample space on the inside and innovative shapes on the outside.

Although traditional cabinets and shelving are still popular today, alternative storage units with unconventional designs are becoming increasingly common. Designers are turning away from traditional concepts in search of new ideas. Their inspiration comes from various sources, such as industrial storage, practical wooden school desks, and the bold shapes of modern architecture.

Mania, designed by Konstantin Grcic, is a prime example of this trend. Despite its slender shape, its spacious interior can store a surprisingly large number of objects. The main body of this piece is divided into five practical drawers, and the entire structure is crowned by an original tray connected with hinges. Mania is made of Multiplex with a maple veneer that has been stained in a white tone. The tray, like the interior of the drawers, is lacquered in matte black.

The second photograph features an elegant model from the Apta collection designed by Antonio Citterio. The main body of this piece has two hinged doors. The two upper shelves attached to the main body have no back piece, which increases their visual lightness.

1 The Mania model.

2 Cabinet from the Apta collection.

2

STYLISH CURIOSITES

problems, Miguel Milà designed the Tomba'l ashtray and umbrella holder. This attractive and practical piece has an exceptionally tasteful appearance. Its main structure is made of iron, which can be painted black or chromed. The ashtray component is made of cast aluminum.

Another handy accessory is the wastepaper basket. The Palau model, designed by Óscar Tusquets Blanca, is an upright square container with openings on all four sides. The wastepaper can be deposited through any of the four openings and falls into a bag held by the pressure of two pivoting stainless steel rods. An aluminum cover

resting on top hides the contents of the bag. This model can also combine an ashtray with the wastepaper basket. In that case, the aluminum cover is placed upside down, forming a basin for ashes and cigarette butts. It also incorporates a grating for putting out cigarettes. This grating is hinged and can be easily swung out of the way to facilitate the cleaning of the ashtray.

Finally, the Bibò model is a laundry cart characterized by its cold, industrial appearance. This cone-shaped design features one large wheel, and rests on a single leg for added stability. It is available with or without an interior bag.

The decor of a room does not always have to be based on daring, innovative pieces of furniture, imaginative arrangements, or ingenious solutions to problems. Often, the decorative style of a house resembles a straight line, without breaks or brusque changes of direction. For those who want to have the best of both worlds and add a touch of state-of-the-art design to their traditional decor, the following pieces will certainly do the trick. Any one of them is enough to brighten up an otherwise dull room.

The first photograph shows the Luna cart designed by T. Colzani. Two pieces of solid cherry wood with large wheels hold two panes of transparent glass. The wooden frame is capped with two chromed metal handles.

An ashtray is an accessory which often goes unnoticed and is often difficult to find when needed. To avoid these

1   The Luna cart.
2   The Tomba'l ashtray and umbrella holder.
3   The Palau wastepaper basket.
4   The Bibò laundry cart.

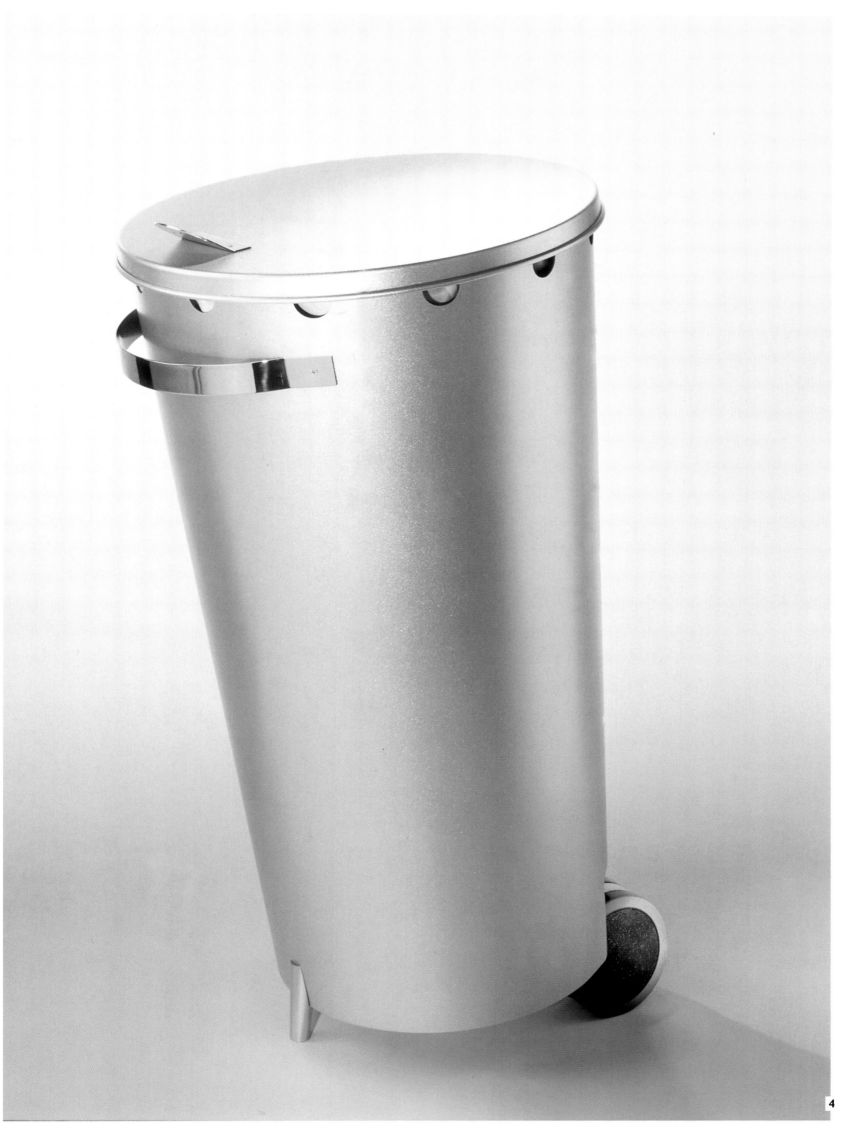

4

CREATING HOME

In order to feel really at home in our place of residence, it is essential to choose furniture that goes with our personality and our lifestyle. This is the kind of furniture that will accompany us through life and make everyday routines easier. Successful decoration is a matter of choosing the appropriate basic elements and surrounding them with accessories and complements that correspond to our tastes and needs.

The first photograph shows a room decorated with a collection of furniture with exceptional character. A large sofa dominates the room and constitutes the room's focal point. Its high, straight backrest guarantees the utmost in comfort, and its soft yet well-defined contours provide the perfect esthetic touch. Some of the key aspects of this design are the shapely armrests with thick cushions and the attractive pale orange color chosen for the upholstery.

Beside the sofa sits an attractive armchair with a youthful, casual feel. This model has a metal frame which supports a white plastic body. Its most distinguishing feature is its elegant, rounded shape, which unifies the seat, back, and armrests.

The center of the room is occupied by a streamlined metal table composed of four slender cylindrical legs which pass through two oval platforms placed one on top of the other. Next to the sofa is an end table with a similar design. This is a smaller version of the model mentioned above, with triangular platforms supported by three legs.

The second photograph features a more surprising and romantic composition. As in the previous example, the sofa is the center of attention. This is a classical model which has

been astutely brought up to date. This design relies on well-balanced curves and features a rounded back which forms one piece with the armrests, as in the classic Chester design. The seat is padded with a single large cushion and has been strewn with several smaller cushions in carefully studied disorder. The legs of this model are hidden behind the upholstery. An elegant, eared armchair flanks the sofa. This classically beautiful piece stands on wooden legs. Both pieces are upholstered in a deep blue tone.

1 The key element in this room is the pale orange sofa.
2 An elegant Chester sofa, flanked by an eared armchair.

1

AVANT-GARDE DESIGN

Daring or innovative designs occupy a special place in many households. Ingenious, often outrageous pieces are designed to shock and to provoke contradictory reactions. Such pieces may seduce by virtue of their uniqueness, or they may invite outright rejection, but under no circumstances will they simply be ignored.

The three models featured here were designed by Timo Salli. The first is Zik Zak, a folding chair with a certain industrial quality. With this design, Salli makes a clean break with the traditional fragility of folding chairs. Zik Zak is anything but fragile. This chair has a rugged, robust, almost indestructible appearance, thanks to its steel frame enshrouded in metal mesh.

Salli created the Tramp lounge chair because he thought that furniture should reveal its inte-

rior as well as its exterior. The metal structure of the Tramp chair is perfectly visible under its nylon slip cover. The translucent slip cover is stretched tightly over the frame and closes with a zipper. Although the chair is fairly voluminous, it gives a light visual effect thanks to this X-ray-like illusion.

The television set often presents a problem in interior design. Gone are the days when it was simply placed in a cabinet or bookcase. An original solution to this problem is provided by Jack in the Box. Jack in the Box is a large, transparent plastic case with a cover and folding arms to hold the television set. The entire mechanism works by remote control, the television set can be raised or lowered, the case opened or closed, and the television turned on or off.

1   *The Zik Zak.*
2   *The Tramp.*
3   *The Jack in the Box model.*

LUXURIOUS INTERIORS

The furniture that graces these pages creates interiors that are remarkable for their serene, modest elegance. Their tasteful beauty has a sober, balanced, and highly attractive effect that is ideal for youthful, informal styles of decor where the accent is on lightness and grace.

The first photograph shows the Benpensante desk, designed by G. Viganò. This robust piece of furniture is characterized by strong, straight lines. It features a desktop covered with black or Bulgarian red leather. The work surface includes built-in holders for pencils and other writing materials. The piece is made of cherry wood and is available in various colors.

Hippo, by T. Colzani, is the ideal writing desk for those who need a large work space. The desktop is supported by two folding supports which feature a rotating mechanism made of solid beech. A personal touch can be added by incorporating metal shelves that can be attached to the supports. This model is made of beech and comes in a variety of colors.

Revolutionary designs may be stylish, but they do not please everyone. For this reason, the Retro P. L. table by T. Zappa and M. Marconato softens its innovative shapes by incorporating a touch of nostalgic classicism. This dining room table features a solid cherry-wood frame which is available in a wide range of colors. The tabletop can be oval or round, and the sinuous metal legs are lacquered in a striking black tone.

Finally, the Minnie couch, designed by T. Colzani, is an attractive model characterized by delicate, feminine shapes. This piece features a solid cherry-wood frame and its seat and back are available upholstered in cloth or velvet. The key elements in this design are the armrests, whose curves are the basis for this model's exceptional gracefulness.

1

2

159

1 The Benpensante desk.
2 The Hippo desk.
3 The Retro P.L. table.
4 The Minnie couch.

MODERN ART

Anyone who believes that there is nothing left to be invented in the world of interior design should take a look at the collection of furniture featured here. These daring and innovative designs delight the senses with their unequaled verve and imagination. They are not only surprising because of their original shapes, but perhaps even more so because of their unique surfaces, which are works of art in themselves.

Thanks to an ingenious process of plastic coating, these pieces of furniture can be adorned with any image. The designers often turn to art for inspiration, reproducing works by Leonardo, Michelangelo, Brueghel, Monet, Van Gogh, Modigliani or Klimt, among others. This plastic-coating process is also used for original works by contemporary painters and offers the possibility of decorating furniture with cloth, photographs, paper, or even dried flowers. Once the piece has been decorated, it is coated with a film of PVC, which protects it from stains and scratches.

What better way to personalize a coffee table than with one's fingerprint? That is exactly what has been done with the model shown in the first photograph. This original and attractive table is the Fingerprint model designed by Fabiana Zanardi.

The second photograph features a table with a strikingly minimalist design. This model is composed of a long, narrow sheet supported by four cone-shaped legs. The tabletop has been decorated with an avant-garde design called Rigature, by Giovanni Zizzi.

Maelstrom represents a step beyond in modern design. Its circular tabletop is elegantly suspended atop the large springs which act as its legs. The surface of this fine example of balance in movement is decorated with a swirling design.

The next design is ideal for the most romantic of interior designs. This simple chest of drawers is decorated with the painting Il bacio, by Klimt. The painting is divided into six practical drawers. The sides of the chest are lacquered in a bright blue tone, and the top is lacquered in white.

The fifth photograph shows an unusual folding screen. Its zigzagging shape is decorated with an extraordinarily beautiful work, Tete, by Modigliani.

4

5

1 The Fingerprint.
2 The Rigature.
3 The Maelstrom.
4 The Il bacio.
5 The Tete.

SUBDUED ELEGANCE

Elegance is the antithesis of excess, which is why it is so often associated with a subdued, understated style. Nevertheless, to be subdued and understated does not necessarily mean boring or conservative. The models featured here are prime examples of how a design can be both sober and innovative at the same time.

Sofas, armchairs, and chaises longues can be divided into two categories. Some are characterized by round shapes and thickly padded surfaces. Others feature straight lines and a more discreet and reserved look. The pieces mentioned here belong in this second category.

The first photograph shows a sofa and chaise longue from the Meteo collection. This line, designed by Luca Meda, possesses a look inspired by the 1950s. The uncluttered contours of this adaptable design give it a slender, airy look that is nevertheless warm and inviting. The back and armrests curve gently in perfect symmetry, and the seat is padded with goose feathers for the ultimate in comfort. Small cushions on the seat provide additional back support. The legs, available in aluminum or wood, rest on streamlined platforms to ensure maximum stability. The Meteo line is available upholstered in various kinds of cloth and leather. The Meteo Due collection, shown in the second photograph, is available only in leather.

The model shown in the third photograph is Bop, a clean design characterized by its short lines and considerable width. The most outstanding feature of this line, however, is its wide range of upholstery offering materials, patterns, and colors for every taste. The designs make extensive use of shadow and light, obtaining an almost infinite range of shades and effects from the colors.

1

2

1 The "Meteo" sofa and armchair.
2 The "Meteo Due" sofa and chaise-longue.
3 The "Bop" armchair.

EASY COMFORT

A comfortable chair, armchair, or sofa is inevitably a result of careful study and design. Once constructed, they undergo thorough testing and analysis to ensure that the finished product is sturdy, durable, and ergonomic. The chairs featured here have successfully passed through all of these stages, as is apparent from their practical and attractive designs.

The first photograph shows the Blitz model designed by Carlo Bimbi and Paolo Romoli. This design is characterized by a practical and balanced appearance especially well suited to offices. It features a tinted or chromed aluminum structure and tubular aluminum legs which are available in anodized, glossy, or opaque finishes. Its seat and back come in recyclable polypropylene, wood, leather, velvet, or cloth.

Storm, by Carlo Bartoli, is notable for the absolute simplicity of its design. Its slender, unfussy contours give this model an air of state-of-the art sophistication. It features a metal frame and a one-piece wooden body without armrests.

Globus, designed by Jesús Gasca is an exceptionally light design which is nevertheless snug and comfortable. The curves on the seat provide the support which is essential for relaxation. It features a frame made of steel tubing which holds a wooden seat and back available in cherry, beech, ash, or maple. Optionally, the seat of this model can be upholstered. This chair can be stacked for easy storage.

The next design is the Split chair designed by Daniele Lo Scalzo Moscheri. This charming and surprising model is characterized by the squat, linear shapes which are the key to its strikingly original look. Its metal structure can be painted in an aluminum tone or lacquered to a pleasant linen white. Its seat and back are available in several woods, such as beech, American cherry, or Canaletto walnut. They can also be upholstered in leather.

1 *The Blitz model with polypropylene body.*
2 *The Blitz model with leather upholstery.*
3 *The Storm chair.*
4 *Globus chairs.*
5 *The Split.*

164

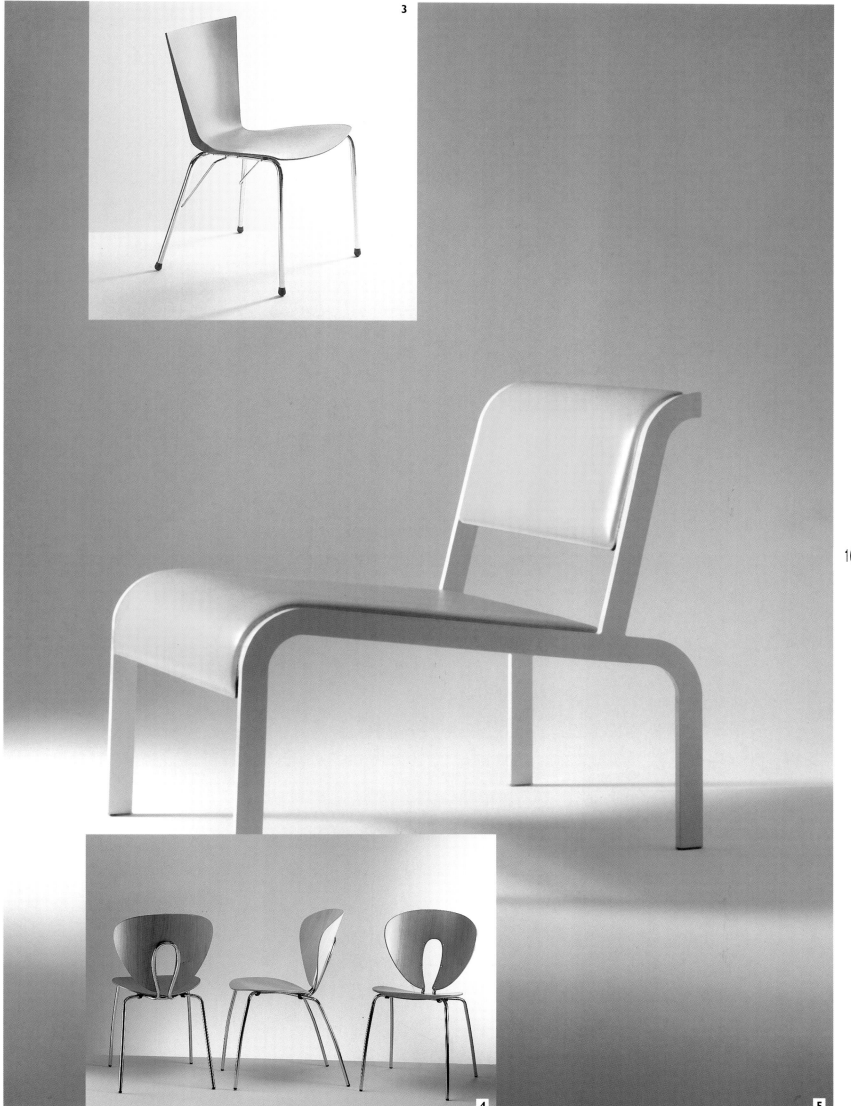

3

165

4

5

SVELTE SEATS

Barstools are among the most unelaborate seats ever designed. Although they are still popular in bars and night clubs, they are also beginning to become an established item in the home, especially with up-do-date, lively, and innovative interior designs. The elegant contours of these pieces add a touch of casual sophistication bordering on the avant-garde. The Jamaica stool, shown here, is an impeccable and harmonious design which also offers a degree of comfort unusual in a stool.

The frame of the Jamaica stool is manufactured in durable chromed steel tubing. Its rotating seat is available in two versions: anodized cast aluminum or solid beech varnished in a natural tone. The line includes low, medium, and high models. The low model is 44 centimeters high (17 inches) and is available with an optional, height-adjustable seat. This model is available with or without wheels. The medium-height model measures 64 centimeters (25 inches), while the high model measures 74 centimeters (29 inches).

The first photograph shows two high Jamaica stools, one with a metal seat and the other with a wooden one. Thanks to the ergonomic design of these seats, the hard surface remains comfortable even after hours of sitting. This model rests gracefully on four simple legs that gradually come together as they near the base. A large metal ring surrounds the legs, and rubber tips on the ends keep the legs from scratching the floor.

The second photograph features a series of Jamaica stools along a bar. These stools are low models with wooden seats. The legs of these stools are different from the high models described above. They descend from the base at an angle before abruptly changing direction just a few inches before reaching the floor. The resulting sharp angle gives the stool a strange, spider-like appearance. This model is also available with wheels.

1 High Jamaica stools with metallic and wooden seats.
2 Low Jamaica stools, without wheels.

LIGHT STRUCTURES

1 The Ovo.
2 The Smoke.
3 The Abici.
4 The Chiara.
5 The Alicante.

The graceful and streamlined models featured here serve a variety of functions and needs, but occupy only a minimum of space. They can all be considered authentic household sculptures which embellish a room with their presence and offer a new concept of interior decoration.

The first photograph shows the Ovo towel rack, designed by M. Marconato and T. Zappa. This slim model is manufactured in metal, and painted white. The rigid bar in the center contrasts with the wavy contours of its arms and legs. A cheerful touch is added by the blocks of cherry wood which decorate the legs and central bar. These blocks are available in a variety of colors.

Smoke, also designed by M. Marconato and T. Zappa, is an original ashtray similar in design to the Ovo towel rack featured above. It is also based on a metal structure which has been painted white, and the ashtray is made of cherry. Blocks of cherry adorn the bar and legs on this model. The wooden elements are available in a wide range of colors.

Stackable tables are pieces which combine an attractive appearance with utmost convenience, since they combine three pieces of furniture in a single, surprisingly compact piece. The third photograph features the exceptionally well-balanced Abici model, designed by P. Silva. These tables fit together with an exceptionally harmonious combination of square and rectangular shapes. The tables are made of cherry lacquered in a variety of colors.

Chiara, designed by T. Colzani, is a display case which features a cherry structure with glass panels. Its greatest distinction is its glass door with rounded corners. The solid wooden posts supporting the glass shelves are another outstanding feature of this model. The shelves can be adjusted to various heights.

In the home, a service cart is often reduced to the function of a stationary display case. For this reason, the Alicante model, designed by G. Azzarello, adds extra functionality to this often underrated piece. This model becomes an indispensable aid in serving food, thanks to its directional wheels and its thoughtful collection of accessories for bottles and tableware. The ingenious mechanism incorporated in the top of this piece allows it to be changed into a table for two persons. The materials used in its construction are natural cherry, natural pith, and metal painted in a textured sand tone.

3

4

5

A WINDOW ON THE FUTURE

The future is just around the corner. The 21st century, which once seemed so far away, is upon us. Technology is advancing at an increasingly startling pace, and what once seemed like science fiction is now humdrum reality. Furniture design, always at the forefront of social life, also plays a role in this process. Contemporary design reflects influences from its surroundings at the same time that it acts as a catalyst for change.

The first two models featured here are examples of how today's design is moving into the future. The Soft Big Easy armchair and the Double Soft Big Easy sofa are two innovative models that make a clean break with the past. These designs possess a wooden or steel frame which supports a body made of polyurethane foam or injected foam. They were designed by Ron Arad for the revolutionary Spring collection.

The Soft Big Easy armchair warmly and gently embraces the person sitting in it. The generously padded body of this chair hides the frame, which disappears under a thick layer of foam. All of the components of this imaginative piece, legs, seat, backrest and armrests, form a single piece, with no visible seams. Straight lines are shunned in favor of wavy curves and round shapes which give the design a decidedly voluptuous and sensual air. The bright electric blue chosen for this model gives it a strong personality based on primary colors.

The Double Soft Big Easy sofa shares the same characteristics of the Soft Big Easy armchair, but doubles its size, turning it into a charming couch. The electric blue color has been substituted by a deep crimson tone, giving it a bold, daring appearance.

Science fiction fans will remember Hal, the computer that drove the crew of an interplanetary spaceship to the brink of insanity in Arthur C. Clarke's novel 2001: A Space Odyssey. In homage to that character, the designer Marc Sadler created the 201 Hal model, an attractive armchair accompanied by a discreet pouf. This piece features a steel structure padded with polyurethane foam and polyester. The upholstery is available in leather or cloth with leather inserts in the back and armrests. A sophisticated mechanism adjusts the position of the armchair.

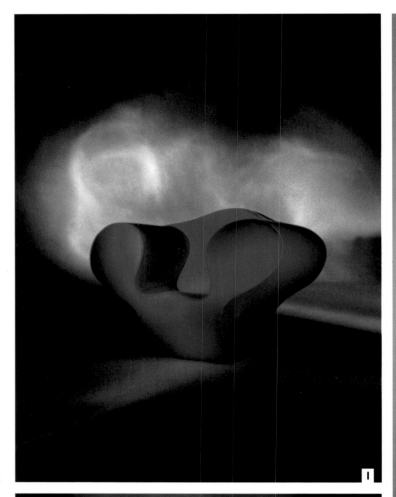

1 The Soft Big Easy armchair.
2 The Double Soft Big Easy
    sofa.
3 The 201 Hal.

SLEEPING LIKE A LOG

A large portion of our life is spent sleeping, and the quality of sleep largely determines how healthy, happy, and efficient we are during the day. Given the importance of sleep, every effort should be made to create a peaceful, relaxing atmosphere that takes our minds off the challenges and troubles of the day. The main component of such an atmosphere is the bed, of course, which should be designed to perfectly fit the body.

The Betty model is an exceptionally attractive and inviting bed that seems to tempt the observer to lie down. Its strong, well-defined lines give this simple, streamlined model a remarkably discrete elegance. This subtle and serene model was designed by Sebastián Bergne. What is most remarkable about this model, however, is not its appearance, but rather what lies under the surface.

The frame of this bed is made of aluminum which has been lacquered in a silvery gray tone. This is protected by a wooden structure which includes the legs and headboard. Support for the mattress is provided by 22 pre-curved slats made of beechwood veneer. The slats have elastic fittings and are placed two by two along the beech veneer frame, which holds them in place. Adjustable slides around the pelvic area ensure perfect support in this section, which normally receives 42 percent of the total body weight. The Betty bed is also available with an upholstered box spring. This option features a softly padded interior equipped with sturdy steel springs. A latex or spring mattress tops off this eminently comfortable model.

For those who prefer a warm ambience with a touch of tradition, there is the Rubirosa bedroom set, designed by Rodolfo Dordoni. The standout piece in this charming bedroom is the elegant bed made of walnut and cherry. The large headboard of this exceptionally beautiful model encompasses two night tables and a shelf with an attractive acid engraving. Two large cushions are placed against the headboard for comfortable nighttime reading.

1 The curved headboard of the Betty bed.
2 The Rubirosa bedroom set.
3 The Betty bed is characterized by its modest elegance..

A BREATH OF FRESH AIR

Sometimes a light, innovative piece of furniture is enough to freshen up a crowded or excessively formal room. The lean designs, light colors, and youthful look of the chairs featured on the following pages are like a breath of fresh air in any room.

The first design shown is the Plec model, designed by Ximo Roca. Plec is a small armchair characterized by its remarkable comfort. Its chromed steel structure is padded with polyurethane foam and the backrest is woven of natural cane pith.

The Creu model, also by Ximo Roca, is a exceptionally classy piece made of chromed steel tubing. This convenient, stackable chair is upholstered in natural wicker, and is available in various colors.

A third model by Ximo Roca, Valle, is characterized by its unusually light design. Its sinuous forms adapt to the body of the user for maximum comfort. This chair can be stacked for convenient storage and features a durable structure made of chromed steel tubing. It is available in a variety of colors to fit any design scheme.

The Lisa chair, designed by Pete Sans is a collection composed of a chair, an armchair, and a stool. The structure of all the pieces is chromed steel tubing and a seat and back upholstered in a weave of natural cane pith. This completely stackable collection is remarkable for both sturdiness and comfort, making it equally suitable for public installations and private residences.

The last model, Bucle, is another chair designed by Ximo Roca. This design also features a frame of chromed steel tubing and natural cane pith upholstery. This chair is available in a wide range of colors and can be easily stacked to save space. This simple, sturdy chair is ideal for both homes and public buildings.

1 The Plec.
2 The Creu.
3 The Valle.
4 The Lisa.
5 The Bucle.

3

4

5

MORE THAN A CLOSET

The Atlante line features a collection of practical, logical, and well-distributed closets that go beyond mere storage space and contribute to the overall decor of their surroundings. These impeccably elegant pieces of furniture possess a calm, reserved beauty which would be an asset to any room. When closed, their doors become attractive polished panels. Inside, their well-organized storage compartments hide a great variety of personal effects.

The Atlante collection, designed by the Kairos studio, is manufactured using only the highest quality materials. The doors are available in the following heights: 124, 134.5, 152, or 159 centimeters (49, 53, 59, or 63 inches). Two-panel doors measure 227 centimeters (89 inches), while three-panel doors measure 259 centimeters (102 inches). The collection is available in several finishes: satin lacquer, natural cherry wood, aluminum, and blue or white glass. The edges and corners for all versions are made of anodized aluminum with a matte finish.

One of the main characteristics of the Atlante collection is the way the external closing system has been differentiated from the interior storage space. The inside of these cabinets comes with a flexible system of vertical racks that can be equipped with a several types of shelves, drawers, and containers. This complex interior is hidden on the outside, however, by large clean panels. This gives the piece a moderately imposing appearance, with only a few horizontal and vertical edges and profiles.

By substituting dividing panels with simple aluminum racks, the collection creates a flexible and innovative system for organizing the interior. The racks hold shelves or rods for hanging clothes. The shelves are available in several finishes, all with a lateral structure of opaque anodized aluminum which attaches to the racks by means of screws.

The closed version of the Atlante closet features a frame with an upside-down "U" shape. The upper section features a rail with an elastic lever for opening the door, which glides on tiny, hidden wheels.

1 Atlante is a collection of practical, attractive closets which blend effortlessly into the surrounding decor.

176

PERFECT PROPORTIONS

A delicate balance of proportion is necessary for a sofa to be at once comfortable and attractive. In fact, this is a general rule for any upholstered furniture, since a lack of balance and proportion will result in an unattractive piece without the inviting look that is so essential to any piece of furniture intended for rest and relaxation. The models featured on the following pages all fulfill these requirements. Each piece is characterized by serenely elegant contours as well as supreme comfort.

The first model shown is Sithya, a sober and tasteful sofa designed by Max Longhi. This large, sturdy piece features a metal frame with elastic straps for suspension. Sithya can be upholstered in leather or a wide range of fabrics. Its pleasant and harmonious contours have a subtly classical look. The rigid base holds three large, soft cushions on the seat, all perfectly designed and remarkably comfortable. The straight back leans slightly towards the rear, and the armrests are perfectly integrated into the whole design, neither too large nor too small. The elegant body of this sofa rests gracefully on simple steel legs with a chrome finish.

The second photograph shows two sofas in an angular arrangement. The bases of both pieces are large rectangular wooden platforms supported by legs of the same material. These platforms hold long, uniform cushions without seams or decoration, which act as seats. One of the cushions leaves space at the end of the platform, in such a way that the uncovered surface serves as an end table. Several large cushions lie against the wall.

A lounge chair with a somewhat colonial look is placed in front of the sofas. This original piece has a wooden frame which is notable for the unique design of its legs. The rear legs rise in a graceful arch which is abruptly broken by the absolutely straight front legs.

178

2

1

1 The Sithya sofa.

2 Elegant sofas placed in an angular arrangement.

MULTIPLE SEATING

Public areas are often equipped with several chairs that actually consist of a number of individual chairs connected to one another. Unlike the cold, uncomfortable models so common in the past, these collective seats bring practicality, elegance, and comfort to public areas, such as waiting rooms, stations, or airport terminals.

The most distinctive characteristic of modern collective chairs is their exceptional lightness. Most of the models are compact, with few components, and with a futuristic appearance verging on minimalist. The materials most commonly used are metal and PVC, although warmer materials, such as wood, are also used.

The first photograph shows the Multi Storm system of modular seating designed by Carlo Bartoli. Two side tables act as dividers and end-pieces of a bar which is available in four lengths: 220, 224, 275, and 305 centimeters (87, 88, 108, and 120 inches). Distributed along the bar are the seats, which are attached by means of metal fittings. The seats are simple and modest in appearance, but sufficiently comfortable. The bar in the center that supports the structure is made of highly resistant chromed steel, while the seats are made of recyclable polypropylene. The seats are available in a wide range of colors, such as red, lavender, white, green, blue, black, coral red, or cream gray.

The second model is Deutsche Bank, a set of chairs designed by Michaela Bisjak, Kai Richter and Markus Graf. This perfectly constructed model evokes the charm and simplicity of rustic furniture. The flexible Deutsche Bank system allows any number of arrangements. The legs of the chair screw onto the base of the rail, which forms the basis for the structure. The seats can then slide from one end of the rail to the other, or be fixed in one position by means of a lever. One of the ends holds a box for depositing small objects. The base, which is available in two sizes, can hold from three to five seats. The legs are made of solid beech, and the seats are finished in maple veneer.

1 The Multi Storm model.
2 The Deutsche Bank model.

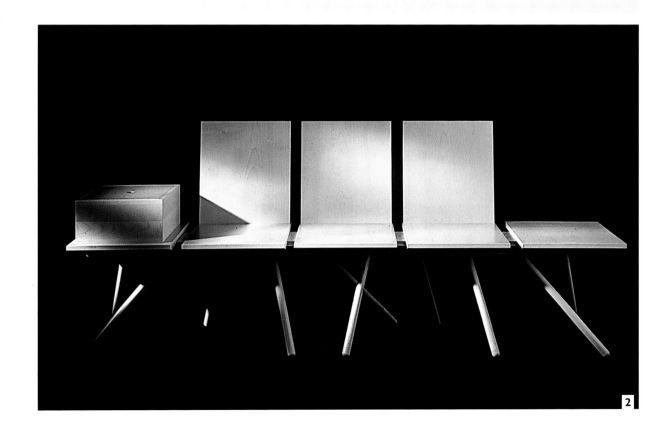

PICTURE-PERFECT BEDROOMS

Although the bed is the undisputed monarch of the bedroom, it is not the only piece of furniture needed for a room to look cozy and intimate. A number of other accessories, such as dressing tables, wardrobes, night tables, and benches, also add warmth and personality to the bedroom.

This section presents the Xen collection designed by Hannes Wettstein. The bed is characterized by calm, straight lines without slants or curves. The structure of the bed is made of beech stained to a cherry finish. The frame serves as support for the mattress, making it unnecessary to add a box spring. The headboard also comes in beech with a cherry finish, and it is available upholstered.

The base of the Xen bed is composed of four boards attached to a metal frame.

Several techniques are used to guarantee maximum comfort. The boards are made of several fir strips glued together and attached to the metal frame with special fittings. Thanks to this system, the boards bend slightly with the body weight and then immediately snap back to their original shape. Pieces of rubber keep the boards from touching the metal directly to avoid creaking noises and wear and tear from friction. The boards located directly under the mattress come equipped with soft rubber disks that keep the mattress from sliding. The structure of this bed allows clear visibility of the steel legs, which are lacquered in a silvery gray color.

One of the most outstanding complements to this bed is the elegant chest of three drawers. This model stands on metal legs which are identical to the legs

of the bed. All pieces of this collection share the same structure. The drawers lack handles, which adds to the impeccably streamlined appearance of each piece.

A practical footstool is a welcome addition to any bedroom. The Xen collection includes this simple and streamlined model, which features conveniently removable upholstery.

2

183

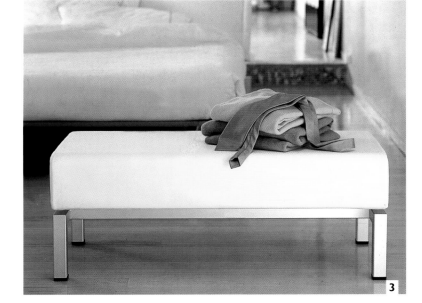

1 Chest of drawers from the
  Xen collection.
2 Bed from the Xen collection.
3 Footstool from the Xen collection.

LIVING ROOM FURNITURE

The living room is usually the social nexus of the home. This room has two main uses, it is a family place for relaxing and socializing, and it is the room that is often used to entertain guests. It is not surprising, it is used more often and by more people than any other part of the home. For this reason it is essential that it be furnished in a practical and organized way that it also be pleasant, harmonious, and appealing. With the proper decoration and furniture, the living room can live up to its name and become a place that is pleasant to live in.

The first photograph shows one example of an elegant and well-designed living room. The star of this room is the spacious sectional sofa, which belongs to the Djune collection. This abundantly cushioned piece has a friendly, inviting, and youthful appearance. The remarkably simple coffee table is composed of a thin rectangular tabletop supported by four sturdy legs. The pleasant appearance of this collection is a result of its reliance on soft tones and high-quality materials. The simplicity of the designs is complemented by exquisite attention to detail.

The components of the Djune sofa are not assembled according to any rigid, predetermined scheme. Each piece retains its own identity and adds personality to the whole. One example of this is the streamlined bookcase on the wall, which combines black and white tones in delicate counterpoint.

The other photographs show several cabinets from the Night-Day collection. These pieces, designed by the Franzolini studio, are characterized by simplicity and clean profiles. This is achieved thanks to carefully selected materials, which include lacquered surfaces, glass, steel, and palm pith. Dark and light colors alternate in carefully planned succession. The pieces in this collection are available in various sizes, and come equipped with several drawers. All the cabinets feature rigid, clearly defined shapes without curves or adornments.

1 A sofa and coffee table from the Djune collection.
2 Various cabinets from the Night-Day collection.
3 Bureau from the Night-Day collection.

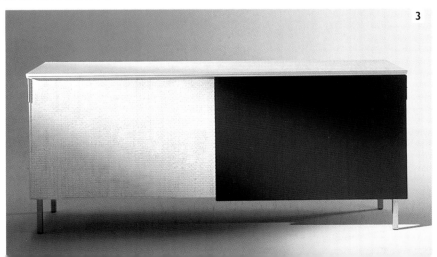

3

UPHOLSTERED CHAIRS

Upholstered chairs and armchairs bring refinement and nobility to living rooms and dining rooms with their distinguished designs. Their forms are inspired by decorative classics from the 18th century, but replace their elaborate, ornate designs with simpler, cleaner lines. The armrests lose their complicated ornamentation and the backs their voluptuous curves.

The Olimpia model, designed by W. Toffoloni, is a balanced and harmonious piece with a soft, calm presence. Its straight, sturdy legs blossom into delicate curves when they turn into armrests. The slightly concave backrest caresses the body in snug comfort. This model features a wooden frame and is upholstered in a youthful blue material. This design is available in the Olimpia/F1 version, with upholstered armrests, and in the Olimpia/PS, with bare armrests.

The Upsala design, by W. Toffoloni and F. Gallinaro, is characterized by the predominance of straight lines, with curves only present in the chair's back. This model serves as a small armchair that provides a maximum of comfort for its compact size. It features a wooden structure upholstered with a refreshing apple-green velvet. The backrest is available with or without upholstery.

The Uni 3 model, designed by Werther Toffoloni, is characterized by a striking, avant-garde design. The elegant and original piece features straight lines softened by slightly slanted legs. The bright upholstery and symmetrical holes decorating the chair's back are the only elements that break up the absolute simplicity of this sober, well-balanced piece.

For a cheerful, informal touch, the obvious choice is the Nex model by Design Ballendat. This innovative and attractive stackable chair features a perfectly round backrest which is completely upholstered, with no visible borders. Its simple structure consists of a rear piece which unites the backrest, front legs, and rear legs in one piece.

1 The Olimpia armchair.
2 The Upsala armchair.
3 The Uni 3 chair.
4 The Nex chair.

3

4

EXCLUSIVE DESIGNS

1 The centerpiece of this bedroom is the
   spacious closet.
2 The headboard of this bed is
   upholstered in bright blue velvet.

In order to create a bedroom that is unique and exclusive, as well as pleasant and intimate, the furniture must have a strong, distinctive personality. The bed should have an elegant and harmonious design that is also daring and innovative. It should be accompanied by several complementary pieces with a strong personality of their own, such as a headboard, night tables, panels, closets, and auxiliary tables. If these pieces are tastefully chosen and combined, the result will be a warm and intimate room with a unique personality.

The furniture featured on the following pages belongs to the Morgante I collection, by the Italian designer

Paolo Piva. Each piece is the result of a state-of-the-art production system based on high-quality materials and attention to detail. The Morgante I bed is an eminently flexible piece that adjusts perfectly to the wall. One of the most outstanding features of this model is its impeccably designed and fully equipped headboard.

The Morgante I bed has a wooden structure that is available in thirty different shades of matte lacquer. The bed measures 167 by 205 centimeters (66 by 81 inches) for a mattress that measures 160 by 200 (63 by 79 inches). It is also available in a larger size: 187 by 215 centimeters (74 by 85 inches) for a mattress measur-

ing 180 by 210 centimeters (709 by 827 inches). The bed is 33 centimeters (13 inches) high. The headboard can be made of American cherry or Italian walnut. Both the bed and headboard can be upholstered in a wide range of fabrics, including velvet.

The first photograph shows several pieces of bedroom furniture. The most striking component is the large closet, which stretches almost from wall to wall. The tall folding doors feature attractive metal trimmings. The side doors are lacquered in white, while the central doors are made of translucent glass. Two small tables stand in the center of the room. These pieces

are made of wood with a single shelf made of translucent glass.

The second photograph features several other pieces from the Morgante I collection. The bed in the center dominates the room with its elegant, balanced shapes and serene beauty. The headboard of this piece is upholstered in bright blue velvet.

THE RIGHT SOFA

Some sofas are soft and abundantly padded, while others are characterized by their sober and seemingly rigid appearance. Some feature sturdy armrests and high, clearly defined backs, while others have softer, more diffuse contours and low backs. The choice of a sofa depends on the use for which it is intended. The ideal sofa for relaxing after a hard day at work can be completely different from a piece intended as a complement to the decor of a living room.

The first photograph shows the Est sofa, designed by Sigla, Bani, Scarzella and Penati. This exceptionally original piece is a far cry from the traditional image of this piece of upholstered furniture. Its most innovative element is the back, which consists of a padded panel attached to the wall. The seat consists of a separate module composed of a metal frame covered with thick padding. The colorful cushions distributed along the back give the sofa a casual, youthful look.

Met is a collection designed by Piero Lissoni and S. Sook Kim that can produce arrangements for any need. The collection includes sofas in three sizes, innovative corner pieces, central modules, end pieces for footrests, armchairs, a bench, and cushions in various shapes and zizes. The Met sofas have a steel structure that can be painted in polished or matte aluminum tones. The padding is composed of polyester and polyurethane foam. The upholstery is completely removable for easy cleaning.

The Moove collection, by Pascal Mourgue, is ideal for a more distinguished style of decoration. The complete collection includes an armchair, three sizes of sofa, a pouf, and a chaise longue with an armrest on the right or the left. Its high back provides unequaled comfort, and the armrests can be adjusted to a more relaxed position. The pieces in this collection feature a steel frame padded with polyester and polyurethane foam. Narrow cushions have been placed against the back for increased comfort. The Moove sofas are available upholstered in leather or a variety of materials. The upholstery is attached with zippers and Velcro so that it can be easily removed for cleaning.

2

1

1 The Est sofa.
2 The Met sofa.
3 The Met sofa and chaise longue.
4 Chaise-longues from the Met collection.

DESIGN AND PRESTIGE

Philippe Starck is one of the most important figures in the world of design. The success of this legendary figure may well be due to his understanding of the importance of imagination in the creative process. More than any other designer, Starck considers that the best designs are the result of imagination which is unfettered by prejudices or limitations.

To illustrate the genius of this renowned designer we have chosen several models from his Cheap Chic collection. All of these pieces are characterized by their economical price, remarkable durability, and unrivaled comfort.

Restraint, distinction, simplicity, and elegance are notions that come readily to mind when contemplating the design featured in the first photograph. The model shown is the Cheap Chic stackable chair, which was presented at the 1997 Milan fair. This piece, which is the origin of the entire collection, features a robust, well-defined metal frame supporting a simple plastic body. Its contours curve just enough to guarantee comfort, avoiding any show of excess or adornment.

Cheap Chic is available in a wide range of colors, including gray, pink, orange, blue, and white.

The second photograph features a model which defies classification. This tall, slender chair is characterized by its surprisingly long legs. Thanks to its unique design, this model is perfect for home bars, since it offers more comfort than the traditional barstool.

Any young, daring style of decor will benefit from the inclusion of the charming tables featured in the third photograph. Their exceptional appeal lies in the cheerful innocence of their soft, rounded contours. A thick, tubular body rests on four attractive cone-shaped legs. The coffee table from the Cheap Chic collection comes in several colors, such as blue, orange, white, and yellow.

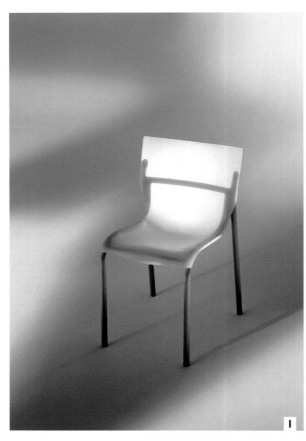

1

2

1 The Cheap Chic chair
2 The Cheap Chic bar chair.
3 Cheap Chic coffee tables.
4 The Cheap Chic chair is available in several colors.

ORDER AND HARMONY

Behind their clean and empty appearance, bedrooms hide a multitude of objects. If the room is to remain clean and uncluttered, it must have enough space for these items to be stored in an organized and convenient way. The bedroom sets featured on the following pages make it easy to fulfill the popular saying "a place for everything and everything in its place."

The Shinto bed, designed by Piero Lissoni, adds new functions to this traditional piece of furniture. The bed can change and grow to fulfill the changing needs of a bedroom. The Shinto bed rests on a simple and streamlined plaque of cherry wood. Various components can be added to this base. These additions include a large headboard with removable upholstery or a cabinet on wheels with a cherry finish or matte lacquer. Other possibilities are the light, uncomplicated night tables that attach to the base of the bed.

For storing clothes or other personal effects, the ideal solution is a large closet like the ones from the Tecnich collection by Piero Lissoni. This collection is the result of exhaustive research into new technologies and materials. It provides a simple and practical solution to storage problems and features a clean, mini-malist appearance. Tecnich Doors, Tecnich Light, and Tecnich Matt constitute three new ways of looking at the notion of a closet. These unique designs are pieces of furniture that can easily adapt to a wide range of needs and circumstances.

Behind its bare, clean exterior, the Tecnich Doors closet hides a spacious and well organized interior. It features convenient doors with special hinges that permit them to open up to 180 degrees. Tecnich Matt, on the other hand, boasts large sliding doors made of cherry wood. The imposing look of these enormous panels is broken up by strips of molding that divide them into sections. This closet is also available with hinged doors in the top section. Finally, the Tecnich Light closet is characterized by its elegant doors, which feature a cherry wood frame and glass surfaces. The glass panels have a look reminiscent of aluminum.

194

1 The Shinto bed.
2 The Tecnich Light closet.
3 The Tecnich Doors closet..

SENSITIVE CRAFTSMANSHIP

The models featured here, most of which were designed by Jaime Tresserra, are all characterized by an exceptionally strong personality. They bring together some of the most laudable of the latest design tendencies, such as traditional craftsmanship, high-quality materials, a Mediterranean feel, contemporary esthetics, and usefulness. Such diverse criteria are successfully combined because of a subtle sense of balance and harmony. The result is a collection of furniture with a magical, timeless quality. These pieces are destined to last forever, without belonging exclusively to any single time or place.

Like a work of art, this furniture appeals directly to the emotions. Most of the pieces are made of white Spanish walnut that has been hand-treated with natural varnish. The metal fittings are brass treated with various methods to obtain several high-quality finishes, such as sulfur, chrome, or silver wash.

The first photograph shows the Imagine headboard by Jaime Tresserra. This piece is made of walnut, and the headrest is cushioned with elegantly folded calf's leather. The metal fittings are chromed and the reading lamps feature a unique design that allows them to disappear into the headboard when not in use.

Next to the headboard is the Imagine night table, also designed by Jaime Tresserra. This design features a stainless steel structure with a walnut tabletop and base. The table boasts two pivoting leather drawers. Due to its innovative design, this table offers a maximum of storage capacity in a minimum of space. The base can be used for stacking books or other objects.

The second photograph features a bed characterized by the extraordinary simplicity of its design. The most outstanding component of this piece is the headboard, with its upholstered surface accented with wooden molding. This elegant piece is accompanied by a svelte night table made of reddish wood. This table features a sparse, basic design with a minimum of components.

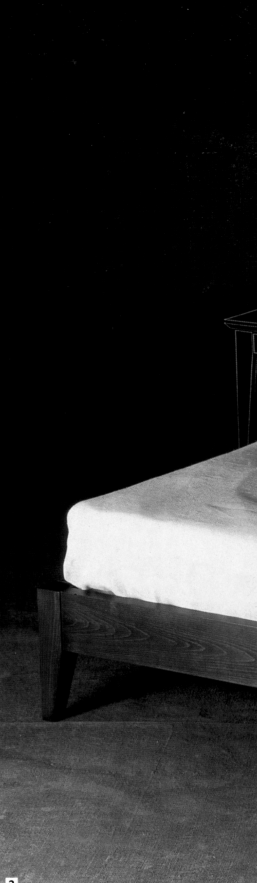

1 The Imagine headboard.
2 An elegant bed characterized by its upholstered headboard.
3 The Imagine night table, closed.
4 The Imagine night table, open.
5 The retractable reading lamp from the Imagine headboard.

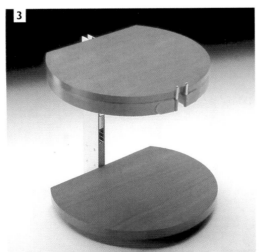

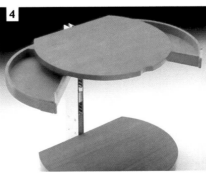

INNOVATIVE LINES

The art of design evolves by breaking rules and experimenting with new shapes, materials, and colors. Creators investigate and try out new ideas which result in unique, innovative designs that are unlike anything that has come before. It is up to the public to decide whether these innovations withstand the test of time and become classic pieces, or whether they fade from memory.

The Apollo lounge chair, designed by R. Lovegrove, is a perfect place to rest and relax. Its snug, cozy contours caress the body and conform to the body's movements, keeping it in a perfect position for total repose. This chair has a simple metal frame which supports a sturdy woven body made of plant fiber. The seat, back,

and armrests are combined in one piece, while a horizontal platform serves as a footrest.

The sinuous, snaking contours of the S chair, designed by Von Dixon and Capellini, seem to defy the laws of gravity. Its main structure consists of a metal circumference with a zigzagging body made of plant fiber. When someone sits on this chair, a perfectly engineered system of counterbalance comes into play.

The model featured in the third photograph is a new version of the S chair described above. This design, by Capellini, shares the same basic structure but is somewhat more elaborate. In this model, the plant fiber body is divided into two

symmetrical halves separated by a pronounced seam.

The 1935 chair, designed by Jean-Michel Frank and Adolphe Chanaux, is based on clean, straight lines. This versatile model fits in with a variety of decorative styles. It features a wooden frame, with a long back and no armrests. The seat and back are made of wickerwork.

1　The Apollo.
2　The S chair.
3　A new version of the S chair.
4　The 1935 chair.

1

THE POWER OF IMAGINATION

Imagination is the quality that is shared by all of the models shown on the following pages. Their shapes possess a striking and unique beauty, and they make use of daring and innovative materials. Even their colors shine with an air of insolence. These designs move decidedly away from traditional tendencies in decoration, and mark what may well become the trends of the future.

The first photograph shows the Tre Onde cabinet designed by Giorgio Pullici. This whimsical design consists of a precise combination of straight lines and sinuous, wavy contours. The smooth, polished top is the only flat surface in this cabinet. The front features two hinged doors whose appearance is softened by three clearly defined convex bulges.

Capitonè Cinque is another Giorgio Pullici design that adapts the esthetics of the Tre Onde cabinet to another piece of furniture. This chest of drawers consists of a svelte, linear body supported by legs that slant slightly outward. Its front is divided into five spacious drawers. The wooden front pieces of the drawers have an original design that is reminiscent of sofa cushions.

The Calypso cabinet, designed by the painter Doriano Modenini, is an extraordinary piece with a youthful, informal, and above all, surprising appearance. Its wooden structure has been painted in a blue tone, and the hinged doors are made of metal. The lower part of the piece holds a spacious drawer, and the front is decorated with various gold-colored adornments.

Finally, Under Control, by Enrico de Paris, is an ideal cabinet for the youngest members of the family. The shape of this piece is similar to that of the Calypso cabinet, but its color is completely different. The rectangular body of the Under Control cabinet has been painted in a soft pastel blue. Like the Calypso model, this cabinet has two hinged doors and a single drawer in the lower section. The most characteristic aspect of this piece is the cheerful decoration on the front panel, which has been inspired by comic books. The Under Control cabinet stands on slender metal legs protected by transparent plastic cylinders.

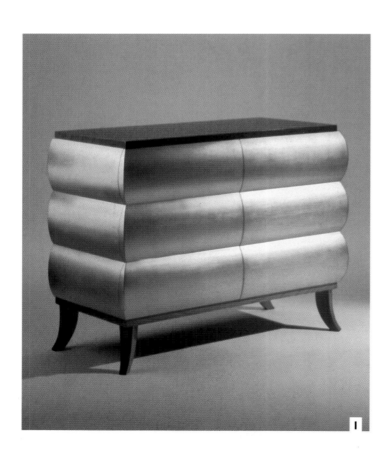

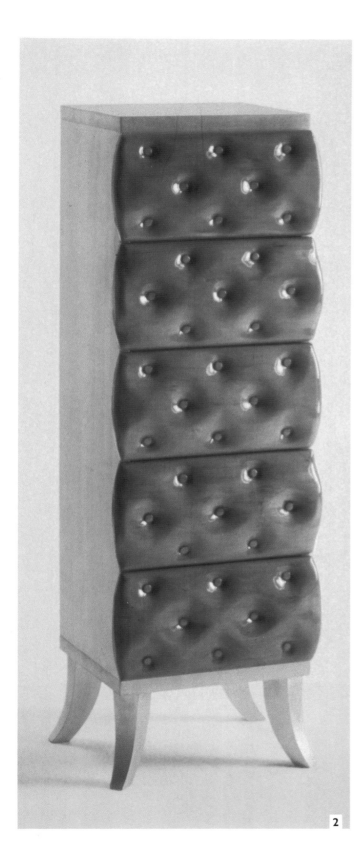

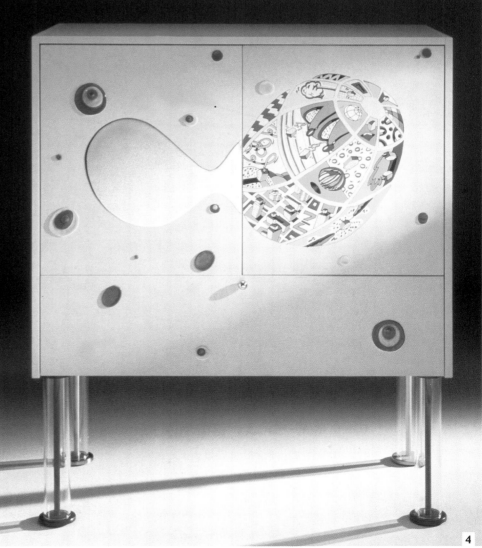

THE RIGHT CHOICE

A sofa is a piece of furniture that reveals much about its owner. A sofa characterized by straight lines and a sober appearance indicates a practical-minded, modest personality. Flowery upholstery and abundant cushions imply a traditional, home-loving nature. However, if the sofa features a daring design, with asymmetrical shapes, wavy contours or bright colors, the owner is probably an imaginative and informal person with a youthful outlook on life.

Fans of innovative, avant-garde design will be attracted by the unique sofas shown in the first photograph. This is the New-Tone model, designed by Massimo Iosa Ghini. Its curved shape is reminiscent of old palatial models. It features a wooden frame padded with polyester fiber and resilient polyurethane foam, which is distributed in various densities for maximum comfort and support. The back is optionally available with goose-down padding. The legs of this sofa are made of aluminum in a polished or satin finish. They are also available in beech that has been stained in a walnut tone. The upholstery of this model is removable for easy cleaning.

The second photograph features a sofa that appears to be inspired by garden furniture. This impression is caused by the metal back and armrests, which are padded with soft cushions.

The Safran model, designed by Vico Magistretti, has an almost minimalist appearance. The padded body rests on a streamlined and elegant frame reminiscent of a tatami. The wooden legs and frame give visual force to the design.

The Box model, designed by Piero Lissoni for the Living collection, is characterized by utmost simplicity. Its structure is made of poplar and spruce, and it is available in several models, making possible limitless combinations, such as corner pieces and modules with or without armrests. The Box comes upholstered in leather or conveniently removable cloth, and is available with chromed legs or an upholstered wooden base.

The fifth photograph shows the Jim model, designed by Enrico Franzolini. This sofa is characterized by clean, rounded lines and a low back. It features a wooden structure covered with polyester fiber and resilient polyurethane foam in various densities. Its legs are available in brass or aluminum.

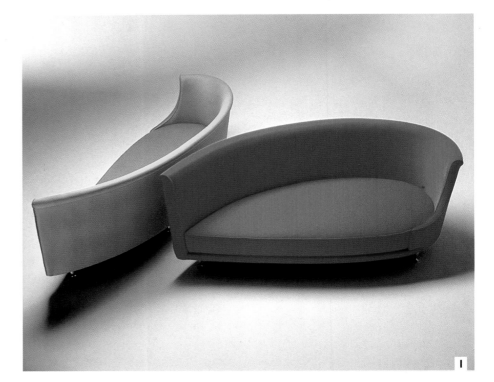

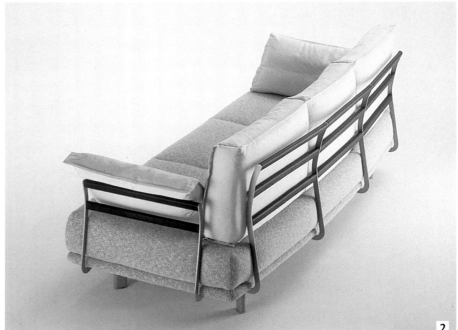

1 The New-Tone.
2 The most characteristic features of this sofa are its metal back and armrests.
3 The Safran.
4 The Box model with upholstered base.
5 The Jim.
6 The Box model with metal legs.

4

5

6

DREAM PARTNERS

1 A bed from the Morgante
  I collection.

2 The XL bed.

3 The Morgante I bed
  attached to a completely
  equipped rear panel.

In order to be comfortable, a king-size bed must be carefully designed. It will, after all, have to provide firm but comfortable support for two people who possibly have different weights and body structures. The latest models offer larger sizes and independent supports for each half of the bed.

The room shown in the first photograph is remarkable for the serene, peaceful atmosphere it creates. The focal point of this room is the Morgante I bed, designed by Paolo Piva. This exceptionally trim and elegant model features a wooden frame, although the body can also be upholstered. The headboard, the most distinctive aspect of the bed, can be ordered with various complements. It can also be upholstered in a broad range of materials, including velvet.

The upholstery is completely removable for easy cleaning.

The second photograph features the XL model designed by Piero Lissoni. As its name suggests, this is an extra large bed, and it is characterized by a minimalist design that gives it a unique personality whose beauty will stand the test of time. Its base consists of a sturdy, wooden plaque that is supported by metal legs. The rectangular wooden headboard seems to be suspended in midair thanks to a nearly magical kind of visual balance. This effect is achieved by strategically hiding the points of contact with the base.

The model featured in the third photograph is another arrangement based on the Morgante I model. The head-

board in this design has been upholstered in an unpretentious white material, and it rests on a panel equipped with several accessories, including night tables, shelves, and drawers in various sizes and styles. Some of the drawers feature front panels made of glass.

2

3

THE EVOLUCION OF UPHOLSTERED FURNITURE

Upholstered furniture is moving away from the classicism that traditionally defines it. This kind of furniture is increasingly moving toward daring, avant-garde designs, bright colors, and vivid patterns. Anything goes, as long as the design remains comfortable. The models featured here are prime examples of this tendency. They will undoubtedly appeal to the most daring decorators.

The most striking features of the model shown in the first photograph are its asymmetrical armrests, one rounded, the other angular. This unique sofa is the Lobby model, designed by the well-known Spanish designer Javier Mariscal. This piece features a steel frame abundantly padded with injected fireproof

polyurethane foam. The rotund and harmonious shapes of this seductive model make it an eye-catching addition to any room.

The Ettorina chair is another design by Javier Mariscal. This youthful, graceful model belongs to the Affectionate Furniture collection. Its silhouette is reminiscent of a charming mouse with red boots. It features a steel structure padded with injected fireproof polyurethane foam.

The piece featured in the third photograph is the Alessandra armchair, another design by Javier Mariscal for the Affectionate Furniture collection. This exceptionally colorful and imaginative design caresses the body with its warm

curves. Its steel structure is covered with injected fireproof polyurethane foam. It stands on stained or lacquered beech legs.

The fourth photograph shows two armchairs from Mariscal's 21 Hotel collection. These chairs are made of the same materials as the Lobby sofa, but have padding that is less obvious. Both models are supported by rotating wheels.

Fans of the most avant-garde trends will undoubtedly be seduced by Saula Marina, another design from Mariscal's Affectionate Furniture collection. Its asymmetrical shapes have a sinuous, aerodynamic look that makes a clean break with tradition. This sofa has a wooden frame covered with resilient polyurethane foam in various densities.

206

1   The Lobby sofa.
2   The Ettorina chair.
3   The Alessandra armchair.
4   Two armchairs from the 21 Hotel collection.
5   The Saula Marina sofa.

4

5